SHE
Tales and thoug[hts...]
adventure Down Under

She'll be right! Tales and thoughts of a woman's motorcycle adventure Down Under. By Chantal Simons

Copyright © Chantal Simons, 2017

All rights reserved. This book or parts thereof may not be reproduced, stored in a retrieval system or transmitted in any form (electronic, mechanical, photocopy, recording or otherwise) without prior permission of the copyright owner. For permission contact:

Chantal Simons
chantal.c.simons@gmail.com
chickonthechookchaser.com

This book is a work of non-fiction based on the experiences and recollections of the author. In some cases the names of people, places, and the details of events have been changed to protect the privacy of those involved.
Due to the dynamic nature of the internet, any links or websites contained in this book may have changed since publication.

Contents

Dedication	1
Map	3
Photo album	5
Prologue	7
Coincidence or Not?	15
The South of the Wild West	26
Eyes on the East	46
Not Flat at All	62
Beach Holidays	76
Happy New Year	87
Green Town	91
The Show Must Go On	101
Sunny Side Up	109
Desolate Deserts and Dust	123
Life Lessons while Looking Like a Racoon	139
A Short Surprising Dip into Civilisation	152
Winding up a Wet West Coast	158
Will We Make it?	173
Destination Darwin	192
Torn in Two	196
Acknowledgements	205
Credit	209

Dedication

To the people, the land and the spirit of Australia.

Map

Photo album

This book will only tell the story in words. To experience the journey in all its vibrant colours, sign up below to get free access to the photo album of She'll be right! Tales and thoughts of a woman's motorcycle adventure Down Under.

http://eepurl.com/cMYJlv

Prologue

From a young age, I always knew that I wanted to ride motorbikes.

My passion began when Dad used to take me for rides on the back of his Suzuki DR650. I was only nine years old but I was hooked from the start by the feeling of the machine moving under my body, the effortless tug of acceleration when Dad opened the throttle. The landscape flew by as the road slipped away beneath us. Instinctively I got into the habit of leaning into corners as we sailed majestically around them. At the same time as I was making these journeys I devoured every bike magazine I could get my hands on, becoming an expert on brands, models, engine sizes and general motorcycle lore. At the age of ten, my not-so-innocent eye was caught by a bright yellow Ducati Monster 600. It was everything I wanted in a bike, combining beauty with power, sleek lines with a ferocious engine. Over the years the vision stayed with me; it was a sight I couldn't un-see. So when at the age of 22, I finally got my licence, I knew just which bike I wanted.

That summer I did my first real road-trip, on the yellow Ducati Monster 620, I dreamed of for years. I went with Rainer, my best friend from high school. It proved a mad mission, a desperate race through nine countries in ten days. From the Netherlands we zipped up through Germany and Poland, crossed the Baltic states, slicing off the tiniest tip of Russia, then travelled by ferry to Sweden before looping back south through Denmark. It wasn't well planned. We just decided to go and a week later threw a set of panniers over the bikes and went. In Germany, we tested the top speeds of the bikes on the autobahn. To my frustration, Rainer won. When I think back to it now, I can't believe the flimsy bags didn't get blown off the bike at two hundred kilometres per hour. On day two my neck already hurt tremendously from being in a race position, but I couldn't have cared less. Upon reaching Estonia, 2,250 kilometres from our starting point, Rainer was the one who had the bright idea to oil the chains. I was totally clueless. No experience with bike mechanics and clearly the wrong bike for the job. But none of that mattered in the slightest. We had an amazing time. And just like that, I was hooked on motorbike travel.

A mere two months later, after successfully

completing my bachelor degree, I needed a break from university life. I couldn't think of a better way to do this than by indulging in two of my all-time passions, motorcycling and travel. After hours poring over an atlas and considering my options, I finally settled on New Zealand as a destination. The Land of the Long White Cloud had a good deal going for it: a language that I could speak and a culture I understood, to start with, while the fact that I was travelling in the European autumn meant it was spring in the southern hemisphere.

Though this trip might not have been quite as impulsive as my jaunt with Rainer, I still had no idea what I was facing. I arrived at Auckland airport with the phone number of some friends of my parents, two large pannier bags and a helmet, beaming with excitement and not quite able to believe I was there as I stepped through a carved wooden entry gate and out into the sunshine of a breezy spring day. Buried in one of the bags was a Lonely Planet I had bought with a gift cheque won with my bachelor research presentation at university. The irony was striking – using a gift from university to get as far away from the place as possible. Twelve time zones away, to be exact, at the opposite end of the world.

It was the first time I had been alone overseas, and along with the excitement and a great sense of inner certainty there was some inevitable trepidation. Two weeks later, however, with loads of help from amazing people, I got underway. Parking my modestly sized behind on the cushiony seat of a Suzuki GS550, wedged between an immense bag of gear and a fully stuffed tank bag, I chased the horizon, travelling from the very top of New Zealand down the very bottom. I passed through forests and valleys, skirted wild coasts and climbed over dizzying mountains, places that left an indelible mark on me. Along the way I met amazing people and had the time of my life.

Tellingly, I fell in love with the bike even though it was nine years older than me and consumed half a litre of oil a day. The poor machine also broke down, on average, every seven hundred kilometres. Over time I collected some meagre knowledge of its inner workings, but I nevertheless ended up spending more money on mechanics then I did on hostels. Finally, after some three thousand kilometres of not-so-loyal service, I had to part with the bike. I could no longer afford to have it repaired. It was a bad break-up. One with tears. One with nights staring at the ceiling going over the what ifs. These two wheels had carried me into a place of freedom that previously had lay out of reach. In the exhilarating but challenging two months we spent together, the bike became part of me. And now I had to carry on alone. I finished the journey around New Zealand by hitchhiking and relocating rental cars. The upside of the rental cars was that you could sleep in them. But I would much rather have had a bike.

Eventually I had to return to university to do my Masters degree. I flew back to the Netherlands. It wasn't easy. I had purposely booked a round trip to New Zealand because I knew deep down, even before I went, that once I got there I would want to stay. I had to be strict on myself, realising that I should finish university before travelling any further. So my rational brain kicked my stubborn ass back to the books, while a piece of my heart was left wallowing in the depths of a pannier somewhere in the far south of New Zealand. It was back to grinding, studying and working my butt off to rebuild my bank account before taking to the road again.

Fast forward a year and a half and I was offered the opportunity to travel to Australia for my final internship. I lived in Melbourne for a year, and quickly felt at home in the country and comfortable with the people. Once again I began to dream of travel. Gradually, in the midst of working, the plan came together to ride around Australia. Despite being happy enough where I was, I desperately longed for the freedom of holding the throttle and just going. I wanted to be reunited with that piece of my heart in the panniers. Eventually the long desired university

She'll be right!

degree slid into my back pocket.

I changed into my bike pants.

The genesis for this book came a little bit later, a mere four months into the journey. By this time I had travelled from the West coast to the East coast of Australia on my motorbike. Here I was on a break from the trip, working and living a stationary life. Because I stayed in close contact with my university background, I was given an opportunity to teach at a university in Brisbane while I lived on the Sunshine Coast. It was a fine summer's afternoon and my flatmate Lisa and I were home for lunch. While Lisa busied herself with pots and pans in the kitchen, I got talking to Amy, a friend of Lisa's, who had come over to spend the day. Amy and I had never met before, but I was drawn to her kind, spirited personality and we immediately got along, sharing stories about ourselves as we lounged on the living room floor of our cosy, light-filled apartment. Suddenly, after listening to one of my stories, about getting bogged on a beach and nearly losing my beloved two-wheeler to the rising tide, Amy's eyes lit up.

'You should write a book,' she declared, excitedly, a note of admiration in her voice.

Taken aback by her enthusiasm, I laughed the idea off.

Prologue

'Nah, I'm not a writer,' I said. 'Why should I write a book?'

I was being entirely honest when I said I didn't want to write a book. Certainly I was flattered that Amy might want to read about my adventures. But back then my stories were simply something to laugh about on a lazy afternoon. I didn't see the point in writing them down and sharing them with the world. Nevertheless, halfway through the journey around Australia (and well before I ever dreamed of crossing Asia), the seed that eventually led to the book you are holding was planted. As the journey unfolded the seed steadily grew, watered and nurtured first by other people and later, under their encouragement, also by myself.

In the course of my journey, two things became increasingly clear to me. The first thing I realised was that people love hearing crazy stories. They crave things that are out of the ordinary, daring, and adventurous. The second thing was that the individuals who embark on these journeys are generally seen as being extraordinarily courageous. Some are even compared to rock stars and superheroes. I find these analogies very flattering, but I don't think they are true. Because people who ride bikes around the world are just people. Maybe they made a few odd choices. Maybe they don't fit the norms. Maybe they are doing things that others so far have only dreamed of. But the truth is, even people who do things that are out of the ordinary, a little bit adventurous, are no different to anyone else. They are happy and sad, powerful and fearful, determined yet full of doubts.

I hope that in reading this book you become part of the journey. I want you to enjoy the crazy and beautiful situations I stumbled upon along the way. I also want to assure you that I'm no more special than anyone else. My aim is to make you laugh and take you to another world. Finally, I want to show you that if I can face the challenges and win the battles that come with embarking on uncertain journeys, then so can you.

Thanks for picking up this book. I hope it will inspire you. Hold on tight and enjoy the ride!

Chapter 1

Coincidence or Not?

It begins like this.

My father, my mother and I are creeping up the east coast of Australia in a small black Nissan Micra. We are just south of Townsville, with me driving, Dad sitting next to me and Mum in the back, surrounded by backpacks and the groceries we picked up in the last town we stopped, when I spot a sign for a lookout. I decide to turn off without consulting my parents and slam on the brakes, taking some heat from Mum, who is violently attacked by a kilo of mandarins. At the top of the hill we get out, grabbing our cameras, and take in the view over the surrounding landscape. It's OK, green fields and the sea in the distance, beautiful but not in a spectacular way. It definitely can't compete with the curves of the fully loaded BMW GS1150 that pulls up behind us. Now *that* is a sight for sore eyes.

We watch as a young man in leathers dismounts,

extracting one leg from between the tank bag and the carefully stacked belongings on the pillion seat before landing with both feet on the ground in a neat hop-skip. He introduces himself, in a thick Scottish accent, as Andrew, and tells us how he has travelled all the way from Perth around the top end of Australia. He is now on his way down the east coast, bound for Sydney.

As he speaks, I look at him in wonder. To me he is like a member of a rare species, a real-life adventurer and a man of great interest. Dad and I are only too eager to pick his brain about his travels. We are soon to embark on an adventure of our own. Andrew, to his credit, is only too happy to share his stories with us. We listen, ears and mouths wide open, as he tells us about the enchanting places he has visited, as well as about the muddy tracks and murky waters he had to conquer in order to reach them. When we share our travel aspirations in return, he tells us with equal enthusiasm how much fuel to carry, what tools we should take and how we should approach the great tyranny of distance. As the conversation evolves, from the corner of my eye I can see that Mum is becoming restless. She is a bona fide member of the four-wheel brigade and would never, under any circumstances, swing her leg over a bike. To calm her down, I promise that we'll get going soon.

Coincidence or Not?

Yet we're all still there, taking pictures of the view, when two women arrive at the lookout and join Dad and Andrew in conversation. When I return to the group I learn that Belle and Nadine rode across Africa on little Honda CT90's. To my delight they explain how they then travelled from London to China on similar machines. Belle's latest adventure, we learn, was a trip to all corners of Australia on a 'postie bike', a kind of everyday contraption that Australia's postmen and women ride when they deliver the mail. The women have visited other places too, but I'm too knocked out with amazement to properly register everything they're telling me. *What are the odds*, I ask myself, *that the three strangers we meet on this lofty hilltop, in the middle of nowhere, are all seasoned motorbike travellers with experience of Australia's massive distances and rugged terrain. Could it be mere coincidence,* I wonder, *or is it something else, rather more uncanny?* Certainly according to the statistical knowledge I have retained from my university days, I know that the likelihood of this random meeting occurring between like-minded folk is zero or less.

The meeting is particularly fortuitous because in the last few months I've been trying to decide on a bike. My plan is to ride around Australia. For this I need something that can go anywhere, on road, gravel, sand, everything. But being one metre fifty-nine centimetres short means that the usual suspects – BMW GS's, KTM's and Suzuki DR's – will leave my feet dangling in mid-air. I've decided that being able to touch the ground while stationary is not only practical, but necessary, so I bring up the issue with my new-found friends. The answer from the done-it-all bikers is unanimous: they suggest either a Yamaha XT250 or a Honda CRF250, or, if I really want ease over speed, says Belle, one of those bright red posties.

The advice is awesome, something I can work with. Meanwhile we continue our conversation, exchanging more crazy stories and great advice. Honestly, we could have stayed there until sunset, happily gabbing away, but after an hour or so we decide to join poor Mum who is waiting patiently by the car. She declares that she has no idea what took us so long, which causes Dad and me to smile between ourselves. With our heads bursting with information and excitement over our upcoming trip, we then all climb back into the cramped little Nissan and get underway.

In the hot and stuffy car both Dad and I are still smiling. In a couple of weeks we are due to set out together on our own epic ride from Perth to Melbourne. I decided that I wanted to ride around Australia while working and studying at university many months ago. It was a logical decision. Riding a motorcycle is my preferred way of discovering foreign countries. The details of the plan evolved slowly but, not long after it was hatched, I came up with the idea of inviting my father to accompany me on at least part of the journey. Dad had recently retired and I had a feeling that he might leap at the chance to join his daughter on a ride. He is, after all, a motorcycle fanatic and the person who introduced me to riding all those years ago.

When I phoned home and asked Mum if she could ask him whether he would be interested, her reply confirmed my suspicions.

'I don't have to ask him,' Mum had said. 'You already know the answer.'

Together Mum, Dad and I fly from Cairns to Perth. Here we pick up a small campervan and set out to explore the coast and parts of the hinterland around the Western Australian capital. The journey proves to be the most fun I've ever had with my parents. It's great to spend time together with them again after living for more than a year at opposite ends of the planet. I enjoy their company and, in my quieter moments, realise just how much I have to thank them for. Ever since I was a child they have given me the freedom to make up my own mind about things and supported me in everything I've ever taken on. Their careful nurturing over the years has endowed me with belief in myself and my abilities and, most importantly I think, given me the confidence to follow my heart.

This morning it's my birthday and my heart is leading me, with Mum and Dad in tow, very firmly in the direction of the local Yamaha store. Just the smell of bike stores makes my heart pump a little faster. They are just so cool. But before we have time to fully immerse ourselves in this amazing mechanical candy shop, we are approached by a slick Yamaha salesman.

'Hello, how can I help you today?' he asks.

In replying I get straight to the point. 'Well, I'm looking for a bike to travel around Australia on,' I say.

He looks up and down the entire 159 centimetres of me and extends his hand saying, 'Hi, I'm Aurelio. You'll need a Yamaha XT250.'

'Yes, that's what we're here for,' I say.

'When are you thinking about leaving?' he asks.

I smile and answer without any hesitation. 'In about four days.'

Aurelio's jaw drops, his slick salesman attitude abandoned like plastic cups on a festival ground, as he marches to the front of the shop, gesturing to us to follow. An XT250 demo bike is parked outside.

'You can try this, you just need to grab a helmet.'

Excited, I run my fingers over the bike. White and black panels surround the tank and the electronics below the seat. A thin blue line details the machine's streamlined shape. The bike has sturdy-looking knobby tyres, a high front fender, and a seat which I find just a little too hard for comfort. It looks to be a good height and tough enough to tackle any terrain. I am instantly smitten.

Meanwhile, Dad has taken a fancy to a black Yamaha XT660. He needs a bike too, after all. It is a few years old but in good nick and ticks all the boxes. Dad really seems to like it. While the bikes are being prepared for a test ride we browse around the shop looking for helmets, gloves, goggles. I make a big deal out of deciding whether to stick with my black bike jacket or, anticipating great heat in the Australian outback, to get mesh motocross armour instead. After weighing the pros and cons of each I decide to stick with the jacket, a decision I will never regret.

Wearing brand new helmets, Dad and I climb enthusiastically on the bikes. After a single lap around the parking lot I realise that the XT250 is a far cry from the Ducati I used to ride. At the same time, however, I experience a strange sense of reassurance when I open the throttle and the bike takes off. This is significant as I was expecting to feel uncomfortable on a new bike, anxious about damaging it somehow, maybe even do something stupid and crash the thing. Yet, amazingly, the 250cc engine seems to listen to every word my brain whispers to it, responding perfectly when I cautiously lean the bike into its first corner and purring with happiness once we get out on the road. There isn't a doubt in my mind. This, I decide with a thrill, is the bike for me. On the way back to the shop I'm already envisioning the adventures that lay ahead, the many kilometres of tarmac and gravel to be covered, the bush camping, the roadside lunches with amazing views.

There is only one problem. Although Aurelio graciously offers to sell the demo bike for a great price, it's still fifteen hundred dollars over my budget. It's a crazy situation. I've just fallen head over heels in love with this mighty iron steed that seems to have been waiting for me to appear. I'm dizzy with enthusiasm for it and consider buying it straight away. But I have to be strict with myself, calculating that fifteen hundred dollars could fund as much as three months of travel. I know there has to be a better way, but for a moment I'm at my wit's end to find it.

Coincidence or Not?

Aurelio, now in full adventure empathy mode, assures me that he totally understands. Before we leave the shop he makes a list of everything we need to look for when buying a second-hand bike, which is what I've decided to do. Dad on the other hand is sold on his XT660 and, as it is within his price range, he has decided to buy it straightaway. Next day he will return to the shop and start the paperwork.

Despite me being unable to afford the bike, Dad and I leave the shop feeling excited and pumped up, ready for adventure. It's my twenty-sixth birthday and I'm skipping and dancing around like a little girl. We are each carrying a new helmet. I have also bought a pair of perfectly fitting Australian-summer-proof gloves.

My priority now is to find the perfect bike. I'm on the lookout for a Yamaha XT250, one that is not too old, with few kilometres on the speedo and, most importantly, a manageable price tag. Possibly it is the kindness of the universe, a birthday present from the travel gods. But miraculously I find the perfect bike. A day after leaving Aurelio's shop, in a suburban backyard, I bestride a second-hand machine and a couple of laps around the local streets are all I need to confirm that it's the bike for me. It is one and a half years old, has done a meagre 950 kilometres and the price is right. It gets the thumbs up from Aurelio whom I quickly consult over the phone.

With the purchase of the bike, the last piece of the puzzle falls into place and I feel fired up and ready to go. We spend our last night together in Fremantle celebrating the end of an amazing family trip and the start of a father-daughter adventure. The next morning Mum flies back to The Netherlands.

Dad buys the two-wheeled black beauty and now, astonishingly, we both have bikes. It takes us another two days of playing around to work out the best possible way to pile our belongings on to our shiny machines. In almost breathless haste we raid the local hardware shop buying jerry cans, tie-downs, bungee cords, waterproof bags, tools, spares and so on. At the campground where we stay we fabricate our luggage systems with imagination, determination, and a solitary Swiss army knife. Under the watchful eye of one of the neighbours our bikes slowly take shape.

'You're true bush mechanics,' the old guy says, saluting us from the door of his tent with a can of beer.

Dad's bike has a top box which provides a solid anchor to tie his dry bag to, on top of which he positions his cans for water and fuel. I dress my two-wheeler with a small suitcase, the kind you take as hand luggage on a plane, zip-tied to the side, and a flat fuel container which serves as a rack for the small mountain of belongings above the pillion seat. It's a balancing act of the highest order, which both amazes and baffles my father.

When Dad first witnesses me piling all the bags on he asks, 'How will you secure that?'

In reply I look at him and, with a beaming smile, say, 'I'll secure it well.'

This, we both know, is exactly the answer he would give and we both start laughing. We are still laughing the next day, when we set out at last on our grand adventure, stopping briefly at the Yamaha shop to thank the boys for their help with a six-pack of beer.

Chapter 2

The South of the Wild West

From Perth we head south along the coast, passing the fancy wine estates and touristy shores of the Margaret River area en route to the far and lonely reaches of the vast red continent. It is a beautiful region with the road passing along the sand-fringed shores of the Indian Ocean and then winding back into forests of amazingly tall karri trees. The trees shoot way up into the sky, rising up to seventy-five metres, opening their leafy canopies high above our heads. The ground beneath them on both sides of the road is thick and lush with all kinds of mysterious plants.

In no time at all we establish a daily routine. Dad wakes up first and prepares his coffee on the little gas stove. As the caffeine hits his brain I crawl out of my nylon home. We eat a quick breakfast and start packing up camp. As soon as the bikes are loaded we hit the road, riding through the morning before stopping at a supermarket to shop for lunch. The squash-proof, no-fridge-required wraps with salami and tomato, which we discover early in our journey, soon become an established noon ritual. In the afternoons we cover more kilometres, heading steadily south, before looking for the perfect spot to camp. We'll explore an area, then, finding what we want, pitch our two little tents which sort of resemble the Sydney opera house, cook dinner, talk or read and finally sleep.

Most nights we stay at the free camping sites scattered along the way. The best of these is right on the beach and incredibly we have it all to ourselves. It is worth a couple of Michelin stars, even if we do have to cook for ourselves, for the roar of the surf in our ears and the sight of the sun sinking into the Indian Ocean. We relax over dinner, but no sooner have we bitten into our couscous and green asparagus than it becomes clear we are no longer alone. From behind a nearby hill sounds the song of bikes, the tin-can metallic ding, ding, ding of two-stroke engines and the high-pitched wailing of small four strokes. The sound amplifies as the local motocross boys tear across the gravel road on to the beach and rip through the sand. We are treated to a dinner show no restaurant can ever compete with.

It's a simple life, full of simple pleasures. And among its virtues is the way it allows my thoughts to wander to corners of my mind that normally go largely unvisited. Up until now, my entire life has been well planned and carefully organised. During my childhood and early youth my daily routine was rather rigid: I'd go to school, play with friends in the afternoons, do my homework and maybe participate in some sport a few nights a week. I had a great childhood, with supportive parents who encouraged me to make my own decisions, like choosing what sports I wanted to do and which school I wanted to attend. Yet the monotony of daily life was a far cry from my dreams of adventure.

Still, even after I'd finished high school, university seemed the logical highway to a good future. As a result of this thinking, those first twenty-odd years of my life were well paved, clearly mapped and properly tested. As I grew older I changed schools several times, which also involved changes in location to a succession of larger cities – no small thing for a girl who had grown up in a small town on the border of the Netherlands and Belgium. In this way every step in my formal education brought with it new challenges in social interaction as well as a small increase in independence.

However after finishing university last month, I was suddenly faced with a freedom of choice that was completely new to me. I had ticked all the necessary boxes. With a university degree in my back pocket I was ready to embark upon adult life. Yet during those years I had been so absorbed by my multitasking, socially active, perfectionist student life that I'd given very little thought to what would come after. There simply hadn't been much time left in my overcrowded, burnout-inducing agenda. Nor, to be honest, had I felt the need to think about the future. So when, therefore, I finally said goodbye to the organised routine of more than seven years of university life, I desperately felt the need to leave all constraints behind. This journey, in other words, is no accident. Moreover, while venturing into the unknown on my bike, the endless roads and empty horizons I encounter spark ever-increasing thoughts about the future. In short, I keep asking myself: what do I want to do next?

I'm also caught up in the excitement of riding with my father. I have this sight in my rear view mirror that is forever carved into my memory: Dad on his bike, just a little dot between the towering trees, powering along the road. It's awesome to be riding with my Dad like this, on an epic journey in a country far from home. Some days I can't quite believe it's happening. The vision of Dad on his bike takes me back to those rides he used to take me on when I was a child, which probably more than most things in my life were influential in me making this journey now.

One day we visit a place called Windy Harbour. It's

running true to form and we battle gale-force sidewinds, zigzagging back and forth across the road, to reach the tiny settlement. After we arrive, and as if the trip to get here wasn't enough of a challenge, I decide it would be fun to take the bike for a spin on the beach. I unload everything before setting off, jokingly telling Dad to start a rescue mission if I'm not back within the hour.

As soon as I turn on to the sand I realise this is a very bad idea. I've never ridden on sand before and it is way too soft. As the wheels churn ineffectively I tell myself that I must keep my speed up. To me it feels like the earth is trying to eat my rear wheel. Every time I slow down the bike begins to sink. Panic kicks in as I face the dilemma of knowing that I need to go back, but that slowing down to turn around will undoubtedly get me stuck.

About a kilometre in, just when things are at their worst, the beach widens and I see my chance. I steer towards the water and nervously pull into a turn, reminding myself that I must maintain speed at all costs. This is a balancing act I haven't performed before, maintaining enough speed to avoid sinking into the sand, while slowing enough not to slip and fall in the turn. I clench the handlebars and launch myself into it, hoping for the best. Halfway through, the rear wheel begins to sink. In a split second it digs itself in entirely. Accelerating only makes things worse – the chain grinds through the sand as the beach swallows half my rear wheel. *Shit.* Desperate now I get off the bike and try revving and pushing it at the same time, but the hole only gets deeper.

I order myself to stay calm. *First things first*, I think, taking off my helmet and sweat-drenched jacket before attempting to lift my beloved machine. To my amazement, the damn thing won't budge an inch. Compared to my Ducati, the XT250 had seemed light and easy to manoeuvre. Now, however, it's like lifting a car.

To make matters worse, the tide is coming in. I stand helplessly by as the first wave washes over my bike. As a second wave approaches, rank panic takes over my thinking. It's a terrible feeling, standing there unable to rescue the bike I've grown so close to in one short week. Suddenly, instinctively, I realise that I need help and, feeling like an absolute idiot, I lean on the horn, tapping out what I believe in my increasingly frantic mind to be Morse code for SOS: three short, sharp blares, two long, three short. The sound carries across the dunes. Beep-beep-beep, beeeep-beeeep, beep-beep-beep… Beep-beep-beep, beeeep-beeeep, beep-beep-beep… Later I'll learn that this actually spells SMS, not SOS, which explains why I feel like I'm honking a ring tone that is vaguely familiar. In any case, with the wind blowing away from the village, and a completely empty beach, I might as well have been in the middle of the desert. No-one, I realise, is ever going to hear this.

As the tide rises, more waves wash over the bike. I have to do something, but what? Remembering some Bear Grylls-type adventure show I've seen, I decide that I need to create traction under the rear wheel. I run around like a headless chicken, collecting a pile of seaweed and kelp from the beach. Then, after digging out a hole to create a ramp-like ascent, I pave the depression with the stuff I've collected. Moving quickly now, I start the bike, put it in gear and push as hard as I can while simultaneously opening the throttle. Momentarily the bike begins to climb upwards; then, in a perfect and spectacular arc the kelp flies from under the wheel, right into the path of an oncoming wave. Sea water fills my boots. *Oh shit, oh shit!* As my feet squelch in the sodden boots, I am suddenly aware of the heat, the sun beating down on my skull, frying a brain that is already overheated with panic. Somehow I have to rescue this beautiful machine, which embodies months of anticipated adventure, from the claws of the rising ocean.

Just as I decide to leave the bike and run back to the village for help, a car appears on the beach. Humans! I jump up and down, wave my arms and honk the horn.

As they turn my way relief floods over me, followed by another wave. Two guys in their twenties leap from the 4x4, beers hand and, to my horror, grinning with amusement. OK, it must have been quite a scene: a bike stuck in the sand, at the mercy of the crashing waves, and this sweaty, clueless, frantic little blonde woman running around in circles trying to set it free.

'How ya goin?' one of the men asks, his grin broadening.

'Well, I could do with some help,' I say.

Clearly entertained by their role as saviours, the two men lift the bike out.

'Where ya going with that bike?' asks the second man, inspecting the out-of-place-looking suitcase zip-tied to the side of the bike.

'I'm travelling around Australia,' I reply, trying hard to sound confident even though I understand how ridiculous it must sound in the current circumstances. I brace myself for laughter, but instead receive an oddly serious look.

'That's not a bike to travel on,' says the first man. 'That's a chook chaser.'

Maybe he is right. Maybe this bike should stay on the farm and chase chickens, instead of carrying me across the country. Or maybe I'm not quite capable of riding around this immense landmass. The incident has rocked my confidence, both in my riding ability and in my capacity to judge the environment. I nod sombrely as I consider the words.

At the same time the tide is still rising, making these existential questions something of a luxury. By now I feel less embarrassed by my situation than terrified of the water and the possibility of getting stuck again. So I convince the guys to drive with me to the beach exit. I get on the bike, shaking, and take a deep breath while they push me to get started.

Don't lose speed, keep that throttle open, don't lose speed, I tell myself, until I make it out of the sand on to the relative safety of the town's gravel road.

I thank the guys for their help and turn into the campsite. Sitting there, relaxed, coffee in hand and utterly unaware of what has happened, I encounter my Dad who asks if I've had fun. I pour out my story and while he's entertained, he's also relieved that our father-daughter adventure didn't finish with my Chook Chaser getting eaten by the rising sea.

Over the following days we visit rugged rock

formations, lookouts with incredible views and endless beaches. The most unbelievable place we visit is Lucky Bay in Cape Le Grand National Park. It doesn't get more Australian than a white beach lapped by crystal-clear blue water and surrounded by rugged red rocks. To top it off there are even kangaroos. On the beach. Among them is a mother with a baby in her pouch. It feels unbelievable seeing this on a beach. The beauty of nature strikes me again and again. I can't get enough of it. My head is spinning. Whenever thoughts of the future creep into my mind this is all I can think of: to ride a bike and experience the unbelievable beauty of the whole wide world. As the days roll by I continue to see myself far away from what is commonly considered civilisation, enriching my being with real experiences and gathering tales and memories from places many people have never heard of.

Saturated by sand and sea, after two mad weeks we turn inland. There is a challenging gravel track, called the Balladonia Road, that connects the coast with the Nullarbor Plain, a vast flat expanse of desert in the middle of the county. Despite my limited off-road experience, we decide to try it. It is one o'clock in the afternoon when the bitumen turns to gravel. Before us lie roughly two hundred kilometres of unsealed road. According to the owner of the last petrol station at this end, we should be able to make it to the other end of the road before dark. But we aren't in that much of a hurry. In fact, we plan to stay the night in an abandoned homestead some two-thirds of the way along. With my beach experience fresh in my mind I expect the worst. My apprehension is increased by the appearance of big signs displaying slogans like '4x4 Only', 'No Caravans', 'No Water or Fuel for the next 194 kilometres'. My trust in a happy ending plummets to near zero.

The first ten kilometres of gravel are a piece of cake. I have the bike going at a steady fifty kilometres per hour and Dad rides comfortably behind me. *This is easy,* I think. *What's the big deal?* We had been warned at the start about the road conditions. It hasn't been graded in twenty years. When it's wet, people told us, it becomes a slip and slide galore and when it's dry it's the bulldust you have to watch out for. If only I knew what bulldust looks like.

Fifteen kilometres in, the road starts to get rougher. Dad is now well behind me. To make the crossing we've loaded up on supplies. Along with tents, sleeping bags, inflatable mattresses and clothes we're carrying between us seventeen litres of spare fuel, another ten litres of water and a lot of extra food. All this stuff is now bouncing around like crazy, rattling and shaking on a road that is gradually getting worse. Surprising myself, I love it at once. *This is what we are here for*, I think. *This is why I got this bike*. Each time I avoid a pothole, the smile on my face grows wider. With every rock I negotiate, my happiness increases. In this rough and tumble way, every kilometre we cover takes us deeper into our adventure. I fall more and more in love with my bike, the surroundings and, most of all, the trip we are on.

Rain has fallen just days before. Big puddles force us to veer from left to right across the road. As we have been warned, the road is covered in the type of dust that assumes ice-rink qualities when it becomes wet. *So this is bulldust.* At one point I become overconfident, riding too fast, so that I find myself with no choice but to go straight through a massive puddle. All I'm thinking is: *Don't brake, don't steer, don't brake, don't steer*, as the bike dips dramatically and muddy brown water shoots up around me. Miraculously I make it through, but with a lot of mud on me.

By four in the afternoon, progressing slowly, we are halfway. We take a break where a side road connects to the main track. A sheet of metal hangs, half attached, to a pole. It used to be a road sign. Beyond this point grass starts to appear in the middle of the road, leaving just two tyre tracks of rocky gravel to ride on. It has been pretty challenging so far, but the best and worst is yet to come.

Just past halfway, our rocky gravel track becomes seriously corrugated. Really, really corrugated. The deepest corrugations I've ever seen, in fact. The bike is jumping around like a bull in a rodeo, determined to throw either me or the luggage. And if this isn't challenging enough, the puddles grow bigger too. We ride on the edge of the road, our handlebars pushing through the branches of the scrub that grows there. Suddenly Dad's handlebars get caught on a bush and he goes slipping and sliding, ending up, after some drama, face down in a puddle. I see this happen in my mirror, but that's nothing compared to all the swearing coming from behind me.

I dismount and run towards him, not sure whether to laugh or cry as I see him clamber out from under the bike. 'Dad, are you OK?' I ask.

'Yeah, yeah,' he replies, 'just these stupid bushes. God damn it. I, well... I took the wrong line. So stupid.'

He limps across the road, away from the mud, where he starts moving his joints and stretching his limbs, an occasional grimace of pain contorting his face.

'Are you sure you're OK?'

'Yes, it's nothing to worry about,' he says, sharply,

like he's annoyed with himself. 'I'll just feel a little sore in the morning.'

That's a relief. But we now face the challenge of lifting a two hundred-kilogram bike, plus gear, out of the mud. Our feet refuse to grip the slippery surface. After a dozen attempts, we reluctantly remove all the gear and, finally, after much pushing and pulling, the tyres touch gravel again. We then pile everything back on to the bike, only to realise that the thing is ridiculously top heavy. Ten litres of water and ten litres of fuel sit like a king and queen on their throne, on top of all the other bags. I feel bad for putting this burden on Dad, but, unfortunately, there is no other way to carry all our supplies.

On the next stretch of road, we have our first close encounter with Australian wildlife. An entire family of emus runs across the road, less than twenty metres ahead of me. Again my thoughts go into overdrive. Trusting my non-existent gravel skills once more, shortly after this I find myself proudly escorted by a female kangaroo and her joey who hop along the road beside me. The experience is both exhilarating and scary and my senses are stretched to the limit the whole time. Don't get me wrong, I love wild animals. However, the idea of making steak out of them with my front wheel is not appealing at all.

As the setting sun turns the sky pink, we reach the abandoned homestead. It stands all alone in the middle of nowhere, a well-deserved home away from home. A neighbouring farmer looks after it, keeping it open so tourists can stay the night. I hurry inside. The place looks as if time has stood still. The wood-fire stove in the kitchen apparently still works. All the appliances and fittings look at least fifty years old. The bedroom is like a museum, complete with a crocheted bedspread and an antique dresser covered with little glass perfume bottles, a pair of long white gloves arranged to one side and a cotton-print dress hanging from the wardrobe door. Checking my dust- and mud-caked face in the ornate mirror, I couldn't have felt more out of place if I'd tried.

Meanwhile from the veranda comes the sound of Dad moving things about.

'I think I've just found an old cylinder head,' he says.

'You found what?' I say and go and look out through the back door, where Dad is standing holding two clumps of rusted metal.

'See, this looks like an old cylinder head,' he says, brandishing one of the pieces, 'and this is a piston rod.'

'That's cool,' I say. 'There's also some old tools over there in that box.'

'They haven't been used for some time, by the look of them,' he says,' casting his eye over the rusty implements.

I drag him inside to show him the house. While I carry on about how charming it is, he, ever practical, goes around tapping his foot on the floorboards and checking the ceilings.

'Do tourists really stay in this place?' he asks, before concluding, 'Well, we should be OK here for the night.'

We cook beans and corn wraps and eat a candlelit dinner. Afterwards we settle down to read our books on the first couch our bodies have encountered in many weeks. The night is peaceful, dreamlike in its silence, and I feel very happy. When at last we crawl into our sleeping bags in the living room, I ask Dad, half-jokingly, 'When you had kids, did you ever imagine that twenty-six years later you would be riding a motorbike with one of them in Australia?'

Dad laughs and even in the dark I can see the twinkle in his eye. 'Not at all,' he replies, 'but I sure don't mind doing it.'

We drift off with big smiles on our faces and sleep like logs. Waking refreshed next morning, we feel confident about finishing off the last bit of rocky road. Once underway Dad, on his poorly loaded bike, has one more go at having a natural facial in the mud. But afterwards we make it without incident to the end, where 1,660 kilometres of bitumen, otherwise known as the Eyre Highway, wait to take us across the Nullarbor.

The literal translation of Nullarbor is 'no tree'. And trees aren't the only things that don't exist on this extraordinary, otherworldly plain. The place is, in fact, quite barren and windswept and the only things we encounter on our crossing are grey nomads, which is what Australians call travelling pensioners, road trains, which are massive trucks that tow two or three individual trailers and move at phenomenal speed, roadhouses, which are petrol stations, and roadkill, which are dead animals that have been run over by road trains.

Being on a motorbike gives you a unique connection with surroundings like this. You immediately notice each change in temperature. You have to hold your breath when road trains throw up clouds of dust into your face. When it rains, there is no way to avoid a drenching. It's a raw connection with the environment and in many ways it's beautiful, although when travelling across a road littered with dead and decaying animals, being able to smell your surroundings turns into a most unpleasant experience. It wasn't until months later that I realised what the whiffs of flesh drying out in this parched Australian landscape reminded me of. The smell of roadkill is exactly the same as the smell of beef jerky. I don't think I can ever again eat beef jerky.

Crossing the Nullarbor is a unique experience. It is almost like a separate country. A country where the roadhouses with their caravan parks are the cities and there are no permanent residents. A country stretching across three different time zones, where cell phones haven't found their way into existence yet and where nothingness is king. In three days we blast through. The road is good but the views are monotonous, blanched earth and withered scrub and a straight line of black tarmac disappearing over the horizon. And, as if riding sixteen hundred-odd kilometres across no man's land isn't crazy enough, stretching across this wilderness is Australia's longest straight road, 146.6 kilometres without a single bend, commonly known as the 'Ninety Mile Straight'. To prevent myself from falling asleep due to boredom, for the entire distance I commit to spotting the camels that many of the bright yellow road signs warn about. Unfortunately without success.

With so little to see and so much ground to cover, my imagination and thoughts have a real ball. Sometimes I think about things like getting stuck at that beach, and question again my decision to navigate my way around one of the largest and least forgiving land masses on earth. I also ponder my future, wondering what I should do when my Australian visa expires at the end of the year. Other times I become all soggy and romantic, my mind meandering into a cascade of daydreams about a guy. Not just any guy, but a guy I've had a crush on for months now. He lives on the other side of the country and we rarely speak. But the time we spent together had such an impact on me that it's not something I've been able to forget.

The truth is I enjoy fantasising about how I might surprise him during my travels. In my head I play out extended romantic scripts. I show up at his workplace, a tour company, and book a runaway trip for two. Or, with the help of his friend, I appear unexpectedly on the beach when they get back from a surf session. In yet another scenario I park the bike in front of his house, knock on the door and ask for a place to sleep. I fantasise endlessly, in enormous detail. Every scene has multiple ways in which it could play out, complete with different fictitious conversations. By the end of the treeless desert, there are enough scripts in my head for a year's worth of blockbuster Hollywood romcoms. The question remains, though, if they will ever be made.

Chapter 3

Eyes on the East

After three days, we reach the town of Ceduna which marks the end of the Nullarbor. We spend a night camping close to the beach before making our way down the Eyre Peninsula. Here we walk along beaches and one day I finally bring up the issue that's been on my mind while crossing the Nullarbor.

'Dad, I'm not sure what to do next after travelling around Australia.'

My Father responds exactly as I expect him to. 'I don't know, honey,' he says. 'What do you want to do?'

I explain how I've narrowed it down to three options: remaining in Australia to pursue an academic career, returning to Europe and spending time with my best friend, or continuing my travels elsewhere.

'Well, those are all good options,' he says.

'Yes, but I don't know what to do,' I say, frustrated because this stuff has been churning around in my head for ages now and I'm still confused. It seems simple enough to choose a single course and follow it, but I feel like this one decision is going to influence my entire life and that scares me. 'I don't know which one to choose.'

Dad doesn't reply. He and I have always been close, and maybe share a similar outlook on life, but we don't usually talk about our thoughts and emotions, plans and dreams. It feels tricky, because in spite of this I've always valued my father's opinion on things. After a moment or two I opt for a different strategy.

'Dad, what would you do?' I ask.

At first he doesn't say anything. Then when at last he does reply he stays true to the way he and Mum have always raised me to think for myself and make my own choices. 'It's your life, sweetheart,' he says. 'You have to figure it out.'

So our conversation ends, with me none the wiser, but respectful and appreciative of my parents' philosophy, which will mean increasingly more to me as my journey unfolds.

The Eyre Peninsula is a popular holiday destination and after our talk we join other tourists in exploring the seafood delicacies of South Australia. However, after the miles of emptiness, jumping back on the tourist train doesn't sit well with us and we soon head inland again. Next stop on the map are the Flinders Ranges, a scarcely populated mountain range, full of wildlife, which start some two hundred kilometres north of Adelaide.

As we head up there we stop at a small café for our regular morning coffee. Upon pushing open the squeaky wooden door I notice pictures of windmills and decorative white and blue Dutch tiles covering the walls of the place. A fellow Dutchman, perhaps? We ask the waitress about the unusual decorations. After a few minutes, the owner joins our table. He is indeed of Dutch descent and, although he has lived in Australia his entire life, he still speaks the language.

Outside the temperature has risen well above thirty-five degrees Celsius and reddish dust blows past the window. It's a strange setting in which to be speaking about our home country, a cold and wet place, in our native tongue. But the owner seems delighted to converse in a language he rarely gets the chance to speak. He talks about where his family is from and about his relatives who still live in the Netherlands. From the look of his cafe and the admiration in his voice, he is obviously proud to be Dutch. Never having lived in the country is a detail small enough to be overlooked. We leave the café with a smile and a crucial piece of advice: *Watch out for the emus, because they won't watch out for you.*

Back on the bike, it strikes me how we define our identity based on a specific country. The image we paint about ourselves when we first meet someone or the way we decorate our homes for others to see. You shake someone's hand, tell them your name and the first question you're asked when you're travelling is: 'Where are you from?' Having spent over a year in Australia by now I have picked up a fair bit of the accent. Indeed even before this, when I was travelling in the US, all the Americans I met were convinced that I was Australian until I told them otherwise. To me it was almost a compliment to be thought of as Australian, for it made me a native English speaker and, in my eyes, a pretty laidback person.

Yet here was a man who has lived in outback Australia his entire life, proudly proclaiming himself to be Dutch and eagerly displaying his connection to a faraway land he has visited no more than a few times. I wondered in light of this whether our country of residence or our descent really have anything to do with who we are. In fact, can the question *Where are you from?* even be answered with the name of a single country, state or city? Of course, where we grow up, and with whom, largely gives us our traditions and habits. It means, for instance, that I deem a slice of bread with butter and chocolate sprinkles a normal breakfast. But it doesn't say very much about me as a person. How much of our personality can we really attribute to our nation of origin or that of our parents? And why have some of us such a strong sense of national pride and belonging?

The bikes take us further north into the dusty heat of the outback. Despite my pondering I have very few answers, only more questions. Meanwhile slowly but surely the breathtaking scenery turns my attention outwards again as we leave the paved highway and turn back on to the gravel. The tyres respond to the change of surface and, as the adrenaline surges in my bloodstream, I enter that familiar state of heightened awareness that seems almost like another mode of existence.

With the Dutchman's advice fresh in our minds we take it slowly. Generally when you drive in Australia the worst times for wildlife are dusk, dark and dawn when the kangaroos are most active. Emus, however, play by an entirely different set of rules, being liable to suddenly appear at any hour. Our slow and cautious pace is not only prudent, it also maximises our enjoyment of the stunning scenery we're passing through. The mountains are an intense shade of red with intriguing patterns carved into them. On each side of the road colossal structures of granite soar upwards. In the middle of this beauty we encounter our very first water crossing. The creek that obstructs the track is only about ten centimetres deep and maybe five metres wide, but it is indisputably a water crossing, so worth a tick.

While my gaze is still fixed on the water now running beside the road, some goats jump out from the scrub right in front of our wheels. Moments later, before we've properly recovered from this surprise, an entire family of emus does likewise. A few kilometres later it's the turn of a kangaroo, which, showing total disregard for his nocturnal nature, leaps across our path. With so many jumping, hopping and galloping creatures lurking around every corner we decide to call it a day. We pitch our tents on a hill a kilometre or so outside a small village, watched the whole time by a pair of curious kangaroos. As evening falls the number of spectators increases, with brothers, sisters, cousins and the odd grizzled parent swelling the crowd.

After dinner we are presented with an incredible sunset. The sky turns the most amazing shades of orange, pink and purple the entire 360 degrees around us. We are intrigued and dazzled by the pictures nature keeps painting. Then, when the sunset show ends, the stars take over. There are thousands and thousands of them. The sky forms a perfect dome over our heads, the inky darkness illuminated by millions of tiny sparkling dots. I've never seen a sky like this before and, to enjoy it to the fullest, I decide to put my pillow just outside my tent. Dad is snoring reassuringly in the tent next to me. Gazing up at the eternal lights I fall into a deep dreamy sleep.

When at last we turn back south, more encounters with wildlife await us. One young emu has just been hit by a car and mum and dad emu are standing on the road, not quite understanding what's going on. It's sad to watch this family tragedy unfold and makes me question whether motorised vehicles should even be allowed in national parks full of wildlife. However, right now, there is nothing we can do. Cautiously we continue our journey. The whole day we cap the top speed at sixty kilometres an hour. We successfully avoid colliding with another emu and a couple of kangaroos.

Eventually we leave the Flinders Ranges behind, exchanging their dark rust-red earth for fields covered in yellow wheat that shimmers in the sun, before entering the lush greenery of the Adelaide Hills. The highlight of this pretty mountain maze is a tiny street called Corkscrew Road. We race up the narrow stretch of tarmac, shifting down as we take the hairpin corners, then accelerating into a short straight before braking for the next tight turn. It's only a few kilometres but it's proper hill-climb material. I'm ecstatic and so is Dad.

It's great to watch Dad really getting into it. He rides in front, attacking every corner. The signs advising on speeds are completely wrong and therefore blatantly ignored. We climb and descend, climb and descend, over and over. The closer we get to Adelaide the busier the road becomes. We spot more enthusiasts like us, crazy bikers enjoying the public road as if it were a racetrack. Dad angles his bike into a sharp left corner, with me just behind him. He's going too fast, so loses his bearing and creeps into the middle of the road, skating the white line, just as a bright orange sports car approaches from the other direction. 'Oh shit… no, no, no, no,' I yell, watching in panic as Dad manages to tuck into the corner, while the orange car swerves to the outside. They miss each other by what looks like a couple of millimetres and my heart is pounding, out of control, ready to leap from my chest.

On the rest of the hills we are more cautious. Besides the challenging riding, this place is impossible to navigate. Roads loop back on themselves. Turnoffs are hidden in corners or behind houses or trees. The only signs we see point exactly where we don't want to go. The map is of little help, and anyway looking at it while riding is a suicide mission in itself. The only solution is to stop and ask for directions, which we do many times. Eventually, with great relief, we find our way out of this beautiful but lethal maze and head for the coast.

We continue our coastal life exactly where we left off. Heading eastward, the Southern Ocean lies to our right, while hills rise to our left. Night after night we camp in amazing spots right on the water. It feels like the road is taking us for the ride. This is without question the Zen of motorcycle travel, close to nature, virtually one with the environment, our thoughts in freefall as we hug the road. For me, I understand, it is exactly where I should be and what I should be doing at this point in my life. Far away from the monotony of the known world where everything is square and orderly and not always fun. Gaining a new appreciation for the beauty of nature. Taking the time to feel its grounding powers.

Zipping along like this, we leave South Australia behind and enter the state of Victoria, ready for another scenic highlight. I have read and heard much about Australia's Great Ocean Road and have visited it once before. Along this famous route, which hugs the wild Victorian coast, lie many tourist attractions, including mighty forests and impressive rock formations. Not long past the border this causes us a little inconvenience. Spotting a sign for something that looks interesting, I lose concentration and, a little abruptly, slam on the brakes. Bang! My bike shudders and groans and, just to the left of me, Dad is struggling to stay upright, before either of us can gain control. Then I realise we just crashed into each other. *Shit!*

When at last we become stationary and assess the damage, it becomes apparent that we have been very lucky. Neither of us is hurt, though we are both shaken; and while Dad's bike looks fine, on my bike the suitcase-pannier is broken. My tent, sleeping bag and mattress are forlornly scattered across the road. I can only apologise for my hasty last-minute call.

'It was also my fault,' Dad says, 'for reading a billboard instead of focusing on the road.'

'So we both can say sorry,' I reply, adding, 'If that's the worse that happens on our trip, we should be happy.'

Through riding together for many weeks, Dad and I have grown closer and more understanding of each other's ways. The apologies we exchange after this incident are a matter of habit. There's no need to mend anyone's hurt feelings. From a nearby roadhouse a few people watch intently as we gather my foldable bedroom and set about packing it back on to my bike.

It's clear that we are literally and figuratively a bit shaken up. We park safely on the side of the road and unpack some bags to get to the tools. With spare tie-downs and bungee cords we strap my camping gear back into the broken suitcase. Melbourne is only two days away and this will do until we reach the city.

We complete the rest of the Great Ocean Road without further challenges. The views are stunning. The glistening, deep blue ocean is the perfect backdrop for a road with lovely curvy bends and great zigzagging stretches. Smoothly we lean the bikes from one bend into the next, revelling in the easy fluidity of our progress. On our motorbikes this isn't just a Great Ocean Road. I decide to rename it the Freaking Awesome Ocean Road. Our last night of the trip together we camp at Kenneth River, where koalas doze in the trees above our tents and brightly coloured parrots eat peanuts from our hands.

The following day, on the approach to Melbourne, we stop for lunch at a pretty spot overlooking the ocean. It's a perfect day and as I eat my sandwich it suddenly hits me that for over a year I lived less than two hours away from this beautiful place and yet only visited it once. I had always planned to come down here for weekends, yet I found one excuse after another not to do so. Either I was too busy with study, or I didn't have enough money, or there was no-one to go with or

I didn't have a car.

None of these futile excuses were really valid, but they felt like real issues at the time. An intense feeling of regret overcomes me. *How*, I ask myself, *did I let creating a life take priority over living it?* Somehow I became a master at procrastinating about things that really mattered, allowing myself to be absorbed by day to day stress, so that I eventually forgot about the fun things I planned to do. Regret is an unfamiliar feeling to me and not something I want to cultivate. I feel genuinely down. When I share my thoughts with Dad, he listens quietly until I finish and then replies in his typical Dad manner, 'I wish I could change it for you, honey.'

Usually, riding clears my head of negative thoughts, but even after we're back on the road, with the wheels spinning beneath me and the ocean wind blowing into my open-faced helmet, I can't shake this feeling. Of course, in time the insight will serve its purpose, inspiring and fuelling my later journey, but I don't know this now so can't use it to make myself feel better. Finally I start thinking about what lies up ahead.

Before we started the bike trip, while studying at university, I also worked and lived on a farm outside Melbourne in order to get a second working holiday visa. The Australian government is happy to have backpackers roaming their land for more than one year, but only if they take on three months of manual labour in a rural area to help out with worker shortages there. Graham and Kristina, the owners of the farm I was fortunate enough to work on, were lovely welcoming people and to finish our trip Dad and I decide to pay them a visit. They are pleasantly surprised to see the two fully-loaded bikes enter their premises. We're welcomed like long-lost family and summoned to unpack and stay the night. It feels like coming home and I'm grateful to have such amazing people in my life.

It's also time for Dad and I to say goodbye. After spending a day on the farm he intends to ride back to Perth. From there he will return to the Netherlands while I will continue northward alone.

Before I depart the Chook Chaser needs to be upgraded to carry the extra baggage we have been sharing between us. On top of the luggage I already have, I must now carry a stove, pots and pans, various other cooking equipment and bottles of water. So, like a true do-it-yourself-father-and-daughter team we pay one last visit to Bunnings, the ubiquitous hardware store, where we buy a plastic toolbox, a bunch of zip-ties and a piece of plywood from which we create a makeshift top box for the bike. The broken suitcase is replaced with a shiny new one.

Before he leaves, Dad once more points out the vital aspects of motorbike maintenance. Oil the chain regularly, he says. Tighten it when the slack is more than a few centimetres by undoing the axle bolt, then turn the snail house like metal plates a notch, before resecuring the bolt. The last step, he says, is especially crucial.

Finally the first part of this adventure comes to an end. Dad piles all his belongings on his black two-wheeler. We hug each other tightly, not knowing when we will see each other again.

'What a unique adventure we've had,' we say to each other. 'Father and daughter sharing a love of motorcycles and travel, spending six weeks on bikes together.'

The time has gone by so quickly. Often, when I've been riding along, I've wondered what went on in Dad's mind on those long empty roads. Did he think about the future, like I did? Did he plan what to eat that night, or would he leave that entirely up to me? Did he think about Mum, or maybe about his mother, my grandma?

Usually, when we got off the bikes, we would talk

about what we saw: nature, other vehicles, animals perhaps. Once we talked about him staying longer, but he decided he couldn't remain away from Mum and Grandma over Christmas. Yet really, we never touched on what went on inside our helmets. We never shared our thoughts much before this trip, so I guess starting it now would have been odd. With mixed feelings I watch him disappear at the end of the driveway, an ending and a new beginning at the same time.

In Melbourne, I catch up with friends and go to the university where I studied and worked over the past year. Seeing everyone again brings back all the questions about what I want to do with my life. They're the same thoughts that occupied me the entire length of the Nullarbor and during some boring stretches after that. *Do I want to do a PhD? Do I want to stay in Australia, in Melbourne?* I find the university environment amazing, and the people awesome. I wonder if I should try and stay. But the more I talk to my PhD friends, the more doubtful I become. In the end I decide that maybe this isn't the time to decide. *And anyway, wasn't travelling around Australia, exploring and enjoying the country, this year's priority?*

Funny, but I have no sooner decided to stop worrying about everything, about the future and about Matt, the guy at the other end of Australia, when suddenly and unexpectedly fun walks right through the door. He's tall, dark and muscular, a handsome specimen. The moment our eyes meet, there is an instant connection. Bright blue staring into blue-green. It feels like he is looking directly into me.

His name is Dario. He's Italian and, I soon discover, he breathes passion into everything he does. He's also off-limits, but that doesn't stop me falling for him head over heels. We spend a few days together, knowing that it's all we have. Maybe part of the magic of our encounter is that we have such little time to share. It allows us to become lost in the moment, so that it feels like we're living on our own little planet, far from anything that connects us to the earth, other people or normal life. We spend long nights in endless conversations about travel, about what we want in life, about being yourself and being happy. We stare silently into bonfires, tease each other and joke, watch the stars and dance by moonlight while we're drunk. Neither the future nor the past seem to matter. But, inevitably, towards the end of these crazy few days we are forced to face reality. Dario must stay in Melbourne, while I have to go. Deep down I know that the commitment I made to myself to go around Australia on the Chook Chaser is one that I have to honour.

Chapter 4

Not Flat at All

After the memorable but confusing time in Melbourne, I continue north. My plan is to visit the Gold Coast, Brisbane, the Sunshine Coast and Fraser Island. To balance all these coastal destinations I decide to turn inland a little and travel up along the Great Dividing Range.

This mountain range runs along the entire east coast of Australia. It is the longest mountain range in the world and separates the vast Pacific Ocean from the great red outback. The climate among these lofty, forested mountains is more temperate than the soaring temperatures of the coast. It is heaven for bikers, as no road is straight, no bend the same. I'm riding on my own, solo, just me, the Chook Chaser and the ever-present company of my thoughts. The roads and the views are much more interesting than the monotony of the Nullarbor. Yet my thoughts tend to drift towards the same familiar topics, life and love. Matt lives somewhere in Brisbane, yet after meeting Dario everything seems to have changed. I really like him and knowing that things can't work out between us for many reasons doesn't change that. So now my thoughts are playing ping pong: *Matt, Dario, Matt, Dario...* Is it possible to really like two guys at the same time?

After two days on my own, listening to the endless ballgame in my head, I feel it's time for a beer and a chat with some locals. When, not far from Bathurst, I cruise down the main street of a typical Australian country town I decide it is the perfect place. I pull up in front of the only pub and ask a man if there is a campground nearby. 'No, not really,' comes the reply. But after a few phone calls the owner of the pub grants me permission to pitch the tent behind his establishment.

The pub is the heart of town. Many men and a few women come here after work to have a couple of drinks before heading home. It's a weeknight, and pretty quiet. The arrival of a foreign girl on a motorbike is about as exciting as it gets. The men indulge in conversations that men indulge in all over the world, mostly about sport and about how their wives complain when they come home too late.

When it comes to closing time, which is 8 p.m. on

weekdays, there's suddenly a lot of commotion. Apparently, one of the guys who's just left has been stopped by the police and breath-tested. Drink driving incurs high fines in Australia. Yet, with farms spread out over many miles, driving is inevitably the only way to reach home. Having had a drink or two, or three or four or seven, often doesn't stop people from hoisting themselves into their utes and piloting their vehicles to the place where their dinner is waiting for them. But with the police lurking around the corner and their hard-earned money at stake, everyone now wonders how they're getting home.

Finally the drunkest one of the group stands up and announces, 'I don't care 'bout these bloody coppahs, I'm going home,' before staggering to his car, swerving the entire width of the footpath, and wrenching open the door.

As soon as he slams the door shut a police car with sirens, lights and the lot appears from around the corner. They've obviously been watching. Luckily for the drunk guy, the police can only give him a fine when the keys are in the ignition, and his alcohol-troubled memory doesn't have the slightest clue where his keys are. So all he gets is a lecture from the cops and applause from the remaining pub guests for his entertaining performance.

Not Flat at All

After a comfortable night behind the pub, I'm invited to breakfast at one of the local farms. Over eggs and coffee the farmer tells the sad story of a fellow biker who crashed his bike the day before. The accident happened not far out of town and the man was airlifted to hospital. There's nothing like a good bike crash story before a day of riding. I'll be extra careful today.

Not long after setting out, the advantage of not always pushing the limits becomes clear. I enter a bend doing seventy-five, where ninety kilometres an hour would have been fine. Halfway through the corner, my heart skips a beat – there's a massive wombat in the middle of my lane. It's about a metre long, maybe half a metre tall, and it crawls around on short, stout legs. Cute and mostly harmless, creatures like this become death traps in traffic, notorious for causing even trucks to run off the road.

But that's not all. There are also two cars approaching from the other direction. My heartrate shoots through the roof. Breaking is useless. Steering will accomplish hardly anything. Moving my hips I push down on the left side of the handlebars, leaning the bike away from the obstacles that are fast approaching. Luckily the centrifugal force at this speed permit me to angle the bike just a little more, allowing safe passage on the inside of the corner. *Whoosh, whoosh*, the cars race pass and the wombat is suddenly behind me, the road ahead as empty as ever. With my heart still racing I realise what a close call this was.

It's the first time in my motorcycle-riding existence that I've been made properly aware of the dangers involved. Riders hear stories of accidents, but still we tend to be naive, cocky, thinking ourselves above the laws of nature. I've always managed to convince myself that as long as I ride carefully, I won't become a statistic. Today's event and the realisation it brings, that it can all be over in a second, heightens my appreciation for what I have and what I'm doing.

For the rest of the day I look at the road, my surroundings and the people that cross my path in a different way. I am more grateful and more appreciative. My riding becomes even more careful as I remember the story about the rider who was airlifted to hospital only the day before. The farmer said it was a mystery how he had crashed, that there were no other vehicles involved, and no animals hit. But I now know better and can see how perhaps the same harmless creature crossed the road just in front of him. Perhaps he was going a little faster, pushing himself harder, just enough to topple him over as he corrected his course.

People are quick to judge motorcyclists as reckless adrenaline junkies. But many of us are actually careful and calculating. Admittedly you receive a surge from the neurotransmitters while riding a bike which is impossible to resist. This starts me thinking about why I ride motorbikes, why I put my life on the line more than is strictly necessary. It's a bit like falling in love with the macho bad boy who you know has cheated on his girlfriends before. You're drawn to the danger of him like a moth to fire. It's risky, and you know you shouldn't, yet you are naively convinced you will be fine.

Early evidence confirms your hypothesis, but soon cracks begin to show in the shell of good behaviour. The act of taking risks brings with it a sense of being alive. The chance of death heightens the pleasure of existence. Knowing that a fellow rider was seriously injured only yesterday on the very tarmac passing under my tyres today are the cracks in the shell. For the first time in my life I experience a glimpse of the dark side of biking, becoming acutely aware of the risks of riding, of the risks of this trip. Do the benefits outweigh them?

Like with so many issues in life, my brain can't produce a sensible answer. But my gut and heart can. As the Chook Chaser smoothly finds its way through the windy forest roads throughout the remainder of the day, I feel with my whole body that this is what I should be doing. Yes, there are risks involved, but

She'll be right!

there is much to outweigh them: the freedom, simplicity and lightness of life on the road, the unique depth to which my thoughts descend when I'm riding, the unforgettable encounters with amazing people and the wonderful purity of depending solely on myself and my machine. Again I become strangely, and maybe naively, convinced that I will be fine, that nothing bad will happen to me.

Travelling further north I come across impressive mountain ranges and the greenest grass in the whole of Australia. The road climbs endlessly up and down. The aromas of the forest accompany me and the Chook Chaser on our way. My personal favourite is the peppery scent of the eucalyptus, or gumtree, as they are called in Australia. When I lived in Melbourne there were a few of these trees on our street. Their scent quickly became synonymous with Australia as my new home. Now, these tall and fragrant trees bring a big smile to my face every time I ride past them.

One day I find a beautiful free campsite. It sits next to a small lake and is surrounded by forest. There are a few other campers, each having plenty of space and privacy between the large trunks of the towering trees. For the first time I succeed at making a fire on my own, which keeps my feet warm and the mosquitoes at bay. The next day I have my very first fishing experience at the invitation of a fellow camper.

Later I find myself on a gravel road that becomes increasingly narrow as it goes on. I find it hard to ride on the loose, potholed surface with a fully loaded bike. It's therefore a relief to see the first road sign in ages – perhaps, I think hopefully, there'll be some improvement further on.

Attached to a white wooden post are two painted arrows. One points to the town I've just come from, the other to the town I passed yesterday. I pull up at once, realising that I'm lost. It's one of my worst fears, the idea of not knowing where I am or where to go next, with no-one around to ask. Australia is a vast landmass with literally thousands of miles of no man's land, empty fields and hills and forest tracks that don't see a single vehicle for days on end. From where I'm standing I can see a third track, unmarked, just up ahead. As it is clear that the other two lead in the wrong direction, I hope that this road will take me where I want to go. Wary, but with little choice, I continue riding until I come to a farm.

A cute puppy welcomes me, licking my hands and trying to climb up my leg. I walk to the house and knock on the door, seeing children's toys spread around the yard, muddy boots carelessly kicked off and left on the steps. It's clear that someone has recently been here, but, strangely, no-one answers my knocking.

'Hello, anybody home?' I call out timidly, all of a sudden self-conscious, which is silly because there seems to be nobody around. What would people think of me, I wonder, a lost traveller on their doorstep calling out for help with the family pet following her every move? I feel strange calling out to the empty house, the deserted yard. It's something I've always felt really weird about, calling out to inanimate objects in the hope a human will notice you. Ungrounded fears and insecurities. Like a house and a shed can judge you.

I'm also aware that I'm not getting any further in my quest to figure out my whereabouts. I walk around the large, white wooden house, which remains still and silent. After finding no-one I reunite with the Chook Chaser where I take a little comfort in knowing that the bike carries everything I need to survive. I'm short on water, but even that can be fetched from the nearby creek and boiled if needed. Still uncertain about what to do, or where to go, I pick up the puppy that is still jumping up against my leg.

The energetic presence of my new four-legged friend helps calm me down. Then a few minutes later a farmhand appears from behind the house. He's alone, he explains, taking care of the property while the family is on holiday. After apologising for not being around to help me earlier, he points at the map and describes how I have to go back about sixty kilometres to a turn-off I've missed.

I thank the guy and reluctantly hand over the puppy. I'm not at all a dog lover, but this sweet, bouncy little creature has stolen a piece of my heart. Briefly I imagine strapping a basket on top of the already dangerously high pile of luggage and taking him with me. However stealing someone's pet to cure my sporadic loneliness is a bridge too far. Instead, I say goodbye, start the engine and retrace my tyre tracks.

With the descriptions from the farmhand, I easily find the missed turn-off and the journey continues in the right direction. This time I follow another dirt road straight through the forest. Again, for kilometres on end there are no people, no traffic, nothing. The only living creatures I see are wallabies. Unlike their big cousins, the kangaroos, these wallabies don't obey the general guideline of only hopping around at dusk, dark or dawn. And they don't seem to be scared of the motorbike either. They make it a sport to hop across the road leaving just inches between their furry bodies and my front wheel.

They scare the living daylights out of me as I'm forced

to brake hard, the back wheel sliding from side to side on the sandy surface of the road. It's not just one or two of them, either; no, they bring their entire extended family. Although the possibility of making a wallaby 'barbeque-ready' turns my stomach upside down, I enjoy watching them. They make big leaps, pushing off with their strong back legs, their furry brown coats catching the sunlight. Sometimes the head of a young one pokes out of its mother's pouch. They are beautiful creatures.

Once again I get into a comfortable routine of riding and camping. Around midday most days I stop in a town to pick up supplies and find a nice spot for lunch. When the sun starts to sink, its rays dropping below the peak of my helmet to shine into my eyes, I know it's time to find a place to call home for the night. By now I've made it close to Grafton, a day's ride from the Queensland border. Today, unfortunately, the map doesn't show any promising spots to camp, so I keep riding, enjoying the smooth, winding tarmac, hoping something will turn up. I consider riding the remaining sixty kilometres to town; though when a kangaroo lurches across the road, it's a clear signal that it's time to set up camp. I opt for the first open field I see, scouting the perimeter for a spot that's not visible from the road, but without any luck.

Instead I find a small bus, with a trailer, parked in a

distant corner. When I go over to say hello it seems to be deserted. However, parked next to the bus is a KTM motocross bike. I'm puzzled that anyone would leave that unattended in the middle of a forest, but rather than think about this too much, I get busy setting up camp on a flat stretch of perfectly green grass, clearly visible from the road, but not far away from the other vehicles. I reason that if anything happens I can call out to my neighbours.

While I'm dragging my belongings into the tent my ears are tickled by the whine of a two-stroke engine. Whatever it is, it's rapidly approaching and its rider likes to seriously rev the thing. Moments later a second KTM flies into the field, on it a guy in his thirties with a bit of a belly, wearing a T-shirt, shorts and flip-flops but no helmet. He stops right in front of me, jumps off the bike and asks, 'What are you doing here?'

Instead of countering the question, or asking why the hell he's riding about like a madman without a helmet, I explain where I've come from and where I'm heading, then ask if it's OK to camp here in the field.

He laughs at me. 'That's quite a trip you're doing,' he says. 'Want a beer?'

Before I have a chance to answer, he yells towards the

bus. 'Johnny! Oi Johnny! Where are ya, mate? Grab us some beers, will ya!'

Johnny emerges from the bus. It turns out he's been sleeping. He passes me a Corona and extends his hand. The other guy introduces himself as Scotty. They are here to have a look at some properties, he says. The bikes are a perfect way to check out plots of land and have a bit of fun at the same time.

'Are you hungry?' he asks. 'We have enough for three.'

Johnny disappears to cook dinner, while Scotty and I collect firewood and start a fire. A second round of beers is opened. Johnny turns out to be quite the chef. He serves up delicious noodles, professionally sprinkled with spring onions, on green and purple plastic plates. For dessert, the beers are swapped for home-brew bourbon and coke. When Scotty learns I'm from the Netherlands his face lights up. He's spent some time there, he says, loves the place and still has good friends there. The bourbon and the stories about bikes and travel keep flowing until deep into the night.

Next morning the guys try to convince me to stay, but I want to keep riding. I promise to meet up with them again in a few weeks. For now I'm bound for the Gold Coast, to see some friends from Melbourne. As I wind up and down the mountains my thoughts drift towards Matt and Dario and then back to Matt. The days with Dario in Melbourne have put the situation with Matt in better perspective, but I feel that I still need to see him, if only to figure out why at the mere thought of him I become a weak-kneed, giggling thirteen-year-old girl.

Chapter 5

Beach Holidays

At the town of Murwillumbah I follow the Tweed River eastward. The road winds down from the mountains into the densely-populated Gold Coast area. The lush greens of the countryside give way to dull grey concrete, but beyond that lies the sparkling Pacific Ocean. The Gold Coast is one of Australia's biggest tourist attractions, with its stunning but overcrowded beaches, multiple theme parks and countless restaurants and bars attracting hordes of people every year. From all over the country people drag their tents, barbeques and screaming kids here in search of sun, surf and sand.

The Gold Coast is also the centre of a thriving singles scene, and those who come looking for a mate to procreate with do so in an all-revealing way. Guys walk around in sleeveless tops, showing off their muscles and tattoos to short-skirted girls with bleached hair and impossibly deep cleavages. It's a mating dance that I, fresh off my bike, have no intention to join. Instead, I meet up with my friends and we eat fish and chips while looking out over the turquoise-blue water and afterwards run across the beach and leap into the waves. It has only been a few weeks, but, oh, how I've missed the ocean.

As I lay in the sand, taking great care not be turned lobster-red in my adoration for this life, my phone pings. It's a message from Matt. 'You're welcome at my place, just make yourself at home,' he writes, adding, 'I'll be there tonight, can't wait to see you!'

That afternoon, tingling with anticipation, I ride to Brisbane. Upon arrival in the city I buy a six-pack of beer, which I balance on the already overloaded Chook Chaser, and head to the address I've been given. A pair of board shorts hangs over the porch railing. There's a skateboard next to the door. *Clearly I have come to the right place,* I think as I try the door, which as promised is unlocked.

Inside, the dimly lit residence displays all the traits expected of a house occupied by surfer dudes in their early twenties. There are piles of dishes all over the kitchen, pizza boxes on the floor together with game consoles and empty beer bottles, while coke cans litter the coffee table. Relieved that I've made it to the right house, I nonetheless feel odd being here alone. It's a bit like committing burglary or snooping through your sibling's room in search of their diary.

Curious, and also wanting to make sure this is the right house, I open one of the bedroom doors. The first thing I see is a staggering pile of condoms. Standing in the doorway I also observe a bed and a guitar, plus a few clothes, but nothing to indicate the identity of the owner of the prodigious rubber collection. A little taken aback, I decide to investigate other areas before taking my chances here. Fortunately the second bedroom I enter reveals a little more about its inhabitant: more board shorts, but also whiffs of an aftershave that smells vaguely familiar and some cut-up credit cards with a name. *Yes, I've come to the right place.*

As instructed, I make myself at home. I have a shower, leaving the bathroom door open because the light is broken. I cook some budget traveller's finest noodles and get comfortable with a book on the couch. By eight-thirty, with the sky growing dark, I start to wonder where Matt is. At ten I double check the name on the credit cards. Half an hour later the back door swings open and two guys stumble in. Nayel and Robin nearly have a heart attack when they notice a person in the room.

'Don't worry, it's just me,' I assure them, smiling at

the guys I met seven months before, when I first came to Brisbane.

It's good to finally have some company in the house. We crack open the beers and I ask where Matt is.

'Uhh, he's staying down the coast,' says Robin, carefully avoiding details. 'We'll probably see him tomorrow.'

It seems odd but I sense that Robin is not in the mood to be pressed. A whirlwind of questions and doubts takes over my thinking. *Why would Matt say that he's looking forward to seeing me, then simply not turn up? Did he feel the same as I did after the weekend we spent together? Is he into me at all? Am I into him?* All too quickly things spiral downward, with self-doubt and pessimism taking hold. When it comes to men and feelings, riding a motorbike across the entire length of Australia has done nothing for my confidence.

The next day, after breakfast, we throw the surfboards and bags in the back of Matt's ute, cram together in the cab and cruise down to the Gold Coast. Why Matt's car is at home, but he isn't, is another question that his mates carefully avoid. The sky is bright blue, just like the ocean at Snapper Rocks. The beach, the sun, watching the surfers, this is the life. I feel there is much more to enjoy when I simply give into it and try to stop this endless worrying. From my towel, caressed by the warmth of the sun, I watch the boys. They are persistent, paddling out, being swept away by the current, walking back and paddling out again. I give it a try, but clearly need more lessons and less current. When I walk back to the towels I think of what I would do if Matt walked up at this very moment.

Before falling into daydream number 507, I spot a familiar figure on the boulevard. Confident, nonchalant stride, messy hair, the ever-present board shorts, a black sleeveless shirt. As he looks over he flicks his cigarette away. Our eyes meet. For a split second, I'm teleported back in time. Like debris picked up by a tornado, images of the crazy weekend seven months ago flash before my eyes. Our 'running away together'. Watching sunsets and sunrises, getting drunk, sleeping in the car in the oddest places, feeding each other pizza and strawberries while driving, running around naked in the forest, bonfires and moonlight massages on the beach.

From the look on his face, I sense that his mind has just revisited those same memories. With difficulty I regain control of my faculties and realise that launching into a passionate kiss might be out of place. We haven't really spoken for half a year. I don't know if he had or has a girlfriend. We are both not quite sure how to greet each other. So instead of a movie-style run-up with a twirling kiss, we end up in an awkward half-hug, with a peck on the cheek, before sitting down to talk.

'How's your trip?' he asks, starting the conversation.

'Very good. Australia's so beautiful,' I reply. 'How are you?'

'I'm good,' Matt responds and pauses for a second or two. 'You know we should steal a board from one of the guys and go surfing somewhere else.'

With that he turns our awkward conversation into a plan of action.

When the others come up Matt tosses the keys to the small white car to Robin. 'You guys take the little car,' he says. 'We'll take the ute.'

The boys head back to Brisbane. Against my better judgement, giving in to my gut feeling that something isn't quite right, I ask, 'Who's car is that?'

Matt deadpans my question. 'Just a friend's,' he says, shrugging, like it doesn't mean anything at all.

This confirms my suspicion that something is off, but

no-one is going to let me in on what it is. *Just let it go, it's none of your business,* my inner voice cautions, aiming to convince me, while Matt and I drive further south to surf at a different beach.

We park and change into our swimming gear. From the other side of the car I hear Matt say, 'I have a new tattoo.'

'Oh yeah, where?' I answer, the sound of my voice muffled by my arm as I wrestle into my bikini.

'Just have a look,' he says.

I turn around and there he is, full, frontal, naked. The twinkle in his eyes and the smile on his face say it all. The doubts about whether or not he's seeing someone, whether I'm still into him, or he's still into me, disappear instantaneously. Once we're dressed we grab our towels, but leave the surfboard in the car. There is no point in pretending. Silently we walk, side by side, on to the beach. The further we walk, the more the tension increases. Then suddenly Matt grabs my hand, and saying, 'I've always wanted to do this,' pulls me into the bushes. We push our way through the branches until we're sure we can't be seen from the beach and put down the towels. When at last we kiss it's the release of a build-up that started in my mind months before.

'I've missed you,' Matt whispers in my ear.

It's the perfect ending to months of daydreaming that started way back in Western Australia.

Later we head back to the beach and run into the ocean. We play like little kids, pushing each other under and bodysurfing together on the waves.

'I missed you, too,' I confess, staring into his ocean-blue eyes. The bubble we lived in, that one weekend in May, opens up and starts to suck us in again. However as we get out of the water and make our way to the car we both feel that things have changed. The tingling electricity between us, the magnetic attraction, still exists, but the feeling of total freedom and the easy carelessness are gone.

The next day it's Christmas and what better way to celebrate an Australian Christmas than on the beach. Boards are thrown into the ute and we happily set off, with Matt at the wheel, Nayel with his knees folded into his armpits to accommodate his long legs and me squashed between them.

We no sooner arrive than Matt volunteers to be my surfing teacher for the day. The water is warm and clear, almost silky on my skin. Several metres ahead of us Nayel puts on a show on his board. But Matt and I, squashed on to one narrow piece of polyester-covered foam, spend most of our time laughing and falling off, being dragged away by the current. Around sunset we are out of the water, watching the waves below from the lookout over Rainbow Beach. It looks perfect, the waves neither too big nor too small, and there is no-one out to crash into. Taking in the beauty of the landscape, the opportunity to surf here, I feel like I should be out there in the water, even though my intellect cautions against it – this time of day the risk of shark attacks is highest. For a few brief moments head and heart do battle within me, before my instincts prevail.

'I'm going down,' I say. 'Do you want to come?'

After a few lousy waves, Matt decides it's time for some real surfing. 'This wave is yours,' he says, pushing the board, with me on it, into the path of an oncoming swell.

I paddle like there is a wild animal chasing me. I give it all I have, but I can't stand on the board, and end up flailing hopelessly in the surf. Giving up, however, is no longer part of my vocabulary. Not here, not now. *If I can ride a bike,* I tell myself, *I can ride a wave.*

When the next wave rolls in I go all out. As the

tumbling water catches the board I put my front foot down, and then my back foot. I stand up, feeling the force of Mother Nature, determined but gentle, lift me up and carry me along. The wave is endless, allowing me to steer the board along it as it neatly unfurls, a foaming blue wall wafting me all the way to the beach.

The whole time it feels like I'm living in slow motion, all of my senses filled with beauty and joy. In the water behind me, Matt bellows yells of victory. On the beach some strangers are clapping and whistling. In the last second before stepping off the board, on to the golden beach, I'm overwhelmed by the breathtaking orange and purple sky, the blue water, the palm trees lining the coast and the intense feeling of happiness in my chest. That's it. Just like heroin, I'm hooked after one shot. No more landlocked living, no more thinking about going back to Melbourne. All the thoughts about my thesis, publishing articles, work, a career. All washed away by that one perfect wave.

When I was fifteen, on a grey drizzly day in the Netherlands, I bought a top with a picture of palm trees and a sunset. Back then it was an image too exotic to ever be real. Yet here I am, riding the perfect wave in a dream I never thought I could live. While riding the Chook Chaser I've spent so much time thinking and worrying about what I want to do after my time in Australia comes to an end. As a result, I've often forgotten to enjoy my time here to the fullest. There is no question anymore about where I will spend the next few months. My heart has been captured by the sun, the beach and the waves.

Matt bodysurfs into shore while I perform a victory dance on the beach. What a Christmas present, my first real wave and I rode it all the way in. As we walk back Matt yells to Nayel, 'We did it, we've converted another one.'

Behind the car door, I change back into my cut-off jeans and pull the ten-year-old top, with palm trees silhouetted against a pink and orange sky, over my head. Dreaming is so much better with your eyes open.

Chapter 6

Happy New Year

After Christmas Matt and Nayel take off for a camping trip. Matt promises to call after New Years, but I already have my doubts. We've had fun together, and the spark is still there, but there is no more fire. At least that's how it feels to me. A little troubled, but with no alternative except to wait and see how things work out, I pile my belongings on to the Chook Chaser and set sail for Byron Bay.

Lying just over the NSW border, Byron Bay is a relaxed little beach town and a backpackers' heaven. However the day before New Year's Eve it's jam-packed with people. Being on the road for so long, camping anywhere and everywhere, I have totally forgotten that the summer holidays are in full swing. I arrive to find every campground, and all the hostels, fully booked. This is a setback, no doubt about it. Still, I keep looking and eventually, just out of town, I find a large makeshift campground. There are thousands of people, many of them barely eighteen. I stand in a long line and reluctantly fork over the ridiculous charge of ninety dollars for two nights.

Why am I even here? I ask myself, as I watch a girl carrying a guy with blood on his face into the first aid post. But then I remember that Byron is said to be *the* place to spend New Year's Eve, so I drop my reservations and decide to just go with it.

At the entrance to the campground a large sign lays down the rules. 'No bonfires. No pools. No drugs.' Before I even reach an empty stretch of grass a ute passes me with a tarp in the tray, filled with water and seven guys drinking beer and yelling their heads off. Pool, check. Around the next corner, someone has decided to get rid of his rubbish the easy way and lit the whole pile up. Fire, check. When I finally find a spot, pitch my tent and go over to my new neighbours to say hello, I find a fourteen-year-old boy stuffing a pipe with hash. Blatant disregards for any rules, check.

My neighbours explain that the ground is like a festival, only without organised artists, food stands or beer tents. And, as promised by the kite-high underage pipe-smoker, once the sun goes down the place really comes to life. Parties spring up everywhere, like the magic mushrooms that grow in these parts. There's a great surge of energy and a plethora of different music styles blares out as men try and impress one another with the size of their stereos. After weeks of tranquillity in the mountains and the relatively calm days on the beach, this all takes a bit of getting used to. *But what the heck, it's almost New Year's*, I think. *Why not party it up a bit?*

It also requires a little effort to shake off my well-meaning neighbours, but I relish being on my own again. The lonely riding of the last two months has taught me a new appreciation for solitude. I spend the whole day at the beach, reading, and watching the waves and the surfers. Laughing inwardly at the girls positioning themselves so perfectly on their towels, fishing for rays to upgrade their tan and catch the attention of one of the board-carrying musclemen.

Towards evening I meet a group of French people. They live in Sydney and have come here to celebrate the holidays. Next to the beach we have a great barbeque dinner together, hindered only slightly by the local police who have been instructed to confiscate all alcoholic beverages.

Once we are out of booze, half of it safely in our systems, the remainder in the hands of the law, we head into town. Again I have underestimated the number of people around. The bars are either overflowing or else they charge an exorbitant entrance fee. Luckily for us the best party is on the street. It's hard to locate where the music is coming from until the crowd moves away to reveal a single talented busker. There must be at least a hundred people dancing, barefoot, initiating flash mobs and hugging strangers. It's the best atmosphere ever to enjoy the countdown to the New Year. Seven, six, five, four, three… two…*one*… Happy New Year! Time to welcome new opportunities, challenges and adventures! Welcome, 2015!

Chapter 7

Green Town

My first interesting destination of the new year is Nimbin. I have met many people on the road who've told me stories about the place. Australia's weed capital, they call it. A town where you can supposedly buy the stuff on any street corner. The idea that this illegal substance is traded so freely in Nimbin triggers my curiosity. Coming from the Netherlands I'm used to the availability of this most-sung-about plant. But in Australia the situation is entirely different. *So how come,* I wonder, *law enforcement has no grip on its trade in Nimbin? Is this one small town outside the law? What makes this place so different from the many other villages similarly guarded from the outside world by the lush green barriers of mountainous rainforest?* To try and answer these questions I decide Nimbin is worth a visit.

The map guides me away from the coast, into the hills. Through a network of twisty minor roads I finally find

She'll be right!

the infamous village. Very slowly, taking in as many details as possible, I ride down the main street. The shops and houses are all painted colourfully, though the paint has faded. There is an ample supply of shops selling knick-knacks and handmade jewellery. The people on the streets are a mixture of young blond German backpackers, mostly female, dreadlocked guys in ripped T-shirts and grey-haired hippies who have been here, I guess, since the seventies. The atmosphere, I sense, is so different here from anywhere else in Australia, it's as if I just entered a different country. At the end of the main street, opposite the police station, I turn left and find a campground a few hundred metres down the road.

After pitching my tent I walk back to town to find a supermarket. Again, there is the police station, so obviously present. *How can weed be traded freely here while the cops are literally on the corner?* Before reaching the main road a perfectly polished metallic-blue car with a loud-sounding exhausts pulls up next to me.

'Need a ride?' asks one of the two guys within, both of whom sport gold earrings.

'I'm fine, thanks,' I reply, adding, 'I like to walk.'

I can't help wondering why anyone would offer you a

ride when the town centre is hardly two hundred metres away. When I finally reach it I walk up and down the main drag, but don't find a supermarket. Eventually I reach what looks like the town square, sit down at a wooden picnic table and continue my observations. Nimbin is clearly unlike any other place I've been in Australia, and I want to find out why everyone is so fascinated with it.

Within minutes the guys who offered me a ride appear, putting a six-pack of beer on the table.

'So you came on the motorbike, alone?' one of them asks, twisting open his first beer.

'Yes, I did,' I say, smiling back at him, understanding at once that the reason they offered me a ride was that they were curious. I also realise that nothing goes unnoticed in Nimbin.

Soon more locals arrive. They all get their drinks from the liquor store across the road, and open them up in plain sight of a camera with a huge plaque underneath it depicting the universal sign for 'It is forbidden to drink alcohol here'. When I ask them about it, they laugh and shrug their shoulders.

'The police have better things to do around here,' one of the men explains. 'They don't care about us drinking.'

With that they open another beer and hand it over to me. 'Cheers!'

Gradually more and more people join the gathering. Some of the older hippies bring their drums and start playing. They explain that Friday night is drum night, a weekly street party that brings all the locals together.

'It's a big event,' says someone, grinning.

Then a guy arrives with a girl who's unknown to the others. He is a little fat, has acne, and is obviously the town's favourite object of ridicule. She, on the other hand, is gorgeous. I soon learn that she is twenty-two, comes from East Timor, and now lives in Australia. With her long curly hair, spotless light-brown skin and entire abdominal region exposed, she instantly grabs the attention of the entire male crowd.

It turns into an amicable dick-measuring contest as one by one the men try and convince the girl that they are so much better than the boy with the acne. It is great fun to watch until in the midst of the friendly rivalry a man in his forties appears on the scene. He wears a leather vest and the sides of his head are shaved, leaving a strip of greying blond hair in the middle pulled back in a ponytail. He is the textbook example of bad news and with his arrival the playful atmosphere suddenly changes.

Determinedly he walks straight up to the girl, roughly grabs her wrist and with the words, 'You, home, *now*,' forcefully drags her away from the group.

Everyone can feel the injustice being done. Immediately the guys combust into fury. Testosterone fills the air as some of them discuss going after the couple and teaching the man a lesson. As I watch it becomes clear to me that this town has its own justice system, based on loyalty and collective moral values, enforced by the alpha males of the community.

The calmer members of the group manage to convince the hot heads that it's none of their business. *They aren't locals,* they reason. *We can't enforce our rules upon them.* The episode has shaken us all up and I get into a conversation on the topic with one of the local girls, Inez, and a guy nicknamed Frenchie. This develops into a discussion about morals and values that quickly turns us from complete strangers into close acquaintances, on the way to being friends. We talk till long after midnight, whereupon, drowsy with sleep but still wrapped in conversation, we decide to follow up next day.

When we meet Inez and I stroll the streets, look at the

shops and have lunch. She tells me she's from Melbourne and moved here three years ago. Nimbin's an odd place, she says, but it's also the first place she has ever really felt at home. According to Inez, people don't judge each other here the way they do everywhere else. Although she's only twenty-eight, she has two daughters and an adopted fourteen-year-old girl who could no longer live with her mother.

'People here are fine with that,' she says. 'They allow you to live the way you want. So long as you don't cut into someone's profit,' she adds with a wink, referring to the town's main form of business.

When Frenchie joins us we get on to the subject of tourists. The reason they are transported to this town by the busload is simple – to buy weed and to see the place where you can buy weed. 'We need them, they need us,' says Frenchie.

'Yes, but sometimes they look at us like we're animals in the zoo,' laughs Inez.

When we later sit down in the middle of town I can see what she means. There seems to be an invisible wall between the people who live here and the people who visit. The visitors walk around the streets, timid, apprehensive, but obviously curious. They stare unashamedly at the confident locals for whom this is a way of life. The locals laugh and yell at each other from across the street. They're dressed in the opposite of the latest fashion and the guys often go without shirts. From what Inez has told me, I gather that people who don't fit in anywhere else find like-minded spirits here. In some cases they are very different, but all share a mutual feeling of non-conformity with the world outside their community.

The main street is like their living room. They are at home and they act that way. Tourists view Nimbin as a town of strange concepts and poorly veiled street deals. They appear not to know quite what they are looking at. This becomes clear when a girl points her camera into an alley where the local guys are trading their merchandise. Instantly three people jump out of nowhere, obscuring the view and yelling out, 'No photos! No photos!'

A bit later, when the police leave their headquarters at the end of the main street, the message, 'Taxi's left the station, taxi's left the station,' echoes along the road. Guys run away, jump on bikes or into cars, and leave the scene before the police car has even backed out of the driveway.

I spend one last day in Nimbin. With Frenchie I climb Mount Warning, in the middle of a rainy night, hoping to be the first ones to see today's sunrise from

Australian soil. It feels like a big adventure, hugely entertaining. When we reach the top we take shelter from the falling drops under a wooden bench over which we spread a large black rubbish bag. The situation is ridiculously funny. Yet in an unexpected moment of seriousness, Frenchie confesses, 'Everyone in Nimbin is part of it, except the cops.' Then he smiles, a crooked smile, and says, 'Well, even they are too... sometimes...'

I remark that I'm surprised he spills his secrets so easily.

'Because we all know you're not a cop,' he replies. 'Sure, the risks are great,' he continues, 'but some people make a lot of money out of it. It's all about tricking, outrunning and outplaying the cops. And even if people do get caught, a lot of the time the charges don't stick. A lot of people are born into it. It's the only reality they've ever known.'

As we speak, the rain fades and daylight brightens our surroundings, but the clouds are too thick for us to see the sunrise. It doesn't matter.

After a few days I decide to leave Nimbin. I say goodbye to the locals, thanking them for their hospitality and openness. It has been good fun meeting them. They have shown me a side of Nimbin outsiders rarely see. When I ride through the main street one last time, I think back to the invisible wall analogy. It feels like I'm on neither side of this wall. Instead I'm sitting on top of it, looking down on both sides, seeing locals and tourists alike, able to relate to them equally as human beings. No stamps, no boxes, no separation. I feel extremely privileged.

With the bike running, sweating in my protective gear, I hug Inez and say goodbye. As we part she looks at me and winks.

'Just remember,' she says, 'whoever told you money doesn't grow on trees has never been to Nimbin.'

I ride back to the Gold Coast. Here a friend graciously allows me to stay at her house for a few days while I recover from a serious infection I've picked up. As soon as I'm OK, I set out once again. Matt hasn't called, as expected, so eventually I call him, and we meet for lunch when I ride through Brisbane.

We've barely sat down before he confesses. 'Since New Year's Eve I've been back with my girlfriend,' he says, just like that.

Suddenly all the things that felt odd before, the pieces of the puzzle, fall into place and it all makes sense.

'I can't explain it. I just have to be with her,' he says sheepishly.

'Isn't that what we all want? I'm happy for you,' I manage to say, although on the inside I feel anything but happy.

I finish my food as quickly as possible. My emotional barometer has plummeted. I need to get out of here before the storm hits. I need to get on the bike, I need to ride.

Once that happens and I've got the protection of my helmet, I can hold back no longer. I sob silently, achingly. While lane-filtering my way out of the messy Brisbane traffic, tears collect in the foam of my goggles.

Why? I yell at myself. Why didn't you stay after that first crazy weekend? You had a shot at simple happiness with him. Why did you screw it up? Why did you get on that plane? Why did you fall for him at all? Why, why, why…?

No answer comes back, but I know the solution. I open the throttle and let the wind clear my mind.

Chapter 8

The Show Must Go On

I'm still crazy when I arrive on Bribie Island, where Scotty has invited me to stay with him and Johnny for a while. When he hears the bike approaching he walks out of the shed and like a traffic controller, but without the whistle, he directs the Chook Chaser to its temporary home. As soon as he spots my face he can tell there's trouble.

'You need a drink,' he concludes, bringing out the homebrew bourbon, even though it's only three in the afternoon.

Scotty is living on Bribie temporarily until he finds a new place. From the contents of the shed, I can see why he chooses this over a normal house. The guy owns more motorised vehicles than T-shirts. There is a vintage car, a land cruiser, the bus, two KTM's, an achingly beautiful, shiny black Ducati and a host of other, equally impressive petrol-drinking machines.

Although a serious size, the shed is only just big enough to house it all.

There is a second floor, extending over half of the lower area. Scotty encourages me to make it my bedroom by putting up a hammock. In next to no time, with the help of his friendly company and the trusty bourbon, I begin to feel at home.

We spend our days fixing up the cars and bikes, cooking great food, reading and lazing on the beach. Scotty, the Land Cruiser and I also go on a trip to Fraser Island. It's a stunning place, the endless white beaches, the sea, the blue lakes. We laugh our asses off trying to sit on inflatable swimming tyres to float down Eli Creek. And then we do it again, this time with beers in our hands. We camp on the beach, under the stars. I sleep in the hammock while Scotty creates a bedroom by rolling out his swag on the roof of the car. When I wake next morning, Scotty yells, 'There was a dingo right next to your bed.'

I think he's bluffing until he shows me the photo.

The time on Fraser Island and in Scotty's shed is the perfect chill-time after all the travelling and the impressions I've gathered, to say nothing of the episode with Matt. The time soon comes, though, when I have to think about the future. The semester is coming up and that means work. One day I travel to Brisbane and meet with Gert-Jan, the head of the Exercise Science department at the university. The meeting starts as a casual catch up, but when he mentions he could use someone to teach I'm immediately interested. We come to an arrangement and for the next few months I will be a bike-riding beach bum, working in Brisbane and living and surfing on the Sunshine Coast. A place with a name that, for someone coming from a cold and rainy country, sounds like absolute paradise. Palm trees and sunsets. Living the dream.

During one of my last nights on Bribie Island, when the day's heat has turned the second floor of the shed into an oven, I decide to move to cooler surroundings. Outside on my back on the air mattress, I watch the stars, millions of them, spread across the sky like fine silver dust. Suddenly, like a shooting star, a thought flashes into my head.

Just like that, I know with concrete certainty that I have to keep travelling after this year. My philosophy about life is still evolving. However I'm gradually learning that it's far better to regret the things that you do rather than the things you don't. I realise that I'm still heartbroken over what didn't happen with Matt. The pain of not following my instincts the first time we met remains fresh and raw. It's an open wound

She'll be right!

that, I can't help feeling, will leave a large scar when it finally heals. I want to be through with such mistakes. I don't want to accumulate any more regrets, any more scars.

There and then I decide that I will travel again and live more for the day. The odds are in my favour. I'm still young. I don't own a house or have a stable job or a relationship to restrict me. I am, what's more, a mere stone's throw away from Asia. The last thing I want is to look back on this part of my life in ten or twenty years time and think, *Why on earth didn't I take the opportunity that was offered to me?*

Lying there beneath the stars, the plan is simple and crystal clear. I've got the temporary job at the university to do first, but afterwards, a new adventure awaits.

Before I dive back into the working life I embark on a last little trip. One of my best friends from high school lives in Sydney and we haven't seen each other in years. There's also another Dutch friend who's recently moved to Australia and lives on the way. It's only a thousand kilometres from Brisbane to Sydney, so I decide to ride down there and say hi.

On Australia Day, a big occasion celebrated with a lot of flags, a top-something music countdown on the radio and a lot of beer, I party with a crowd of strangers at a place called Sapphire Beach. I crash out in a spare bed in someone's house and the night ends with a storm which drenches my empty tent, delaying my departure for Sydney for a day. The following day I finally set out and, after an epic ride, the journey proves a great success. After a couple of days spent catching up with friends, exchanging memories and talking about old school and university mates, I'm ready to head back up the coast and start work.

On the way back I ride along the edge of the famous and very beautiful Blue Mountains, then continue north past Newcastle on the motorway. I prefer travelling on smaller roads, but with work waiting for me in Brisbane, I have to cover some ground. At the end of the day I camp close to the highway at a truck stop. There is a bar nearby that looks reasonably appealing so I decide to check it out. Not long after I position my behind on a heavy wooden bar stool one of the younger customers comes over. He is a chef, he tells me, and has worked in several restaurants in Sydney. We have an interesting chat until the owner declares that he is closing up. It's only nine o'clock, too early for bed, so I'm invited for another drink at the chef's house.

When we walk in, his girlfriend is surprised to see a stranger. However she soon becomes curious when she learns about my bike trip. We sit down in the dark living room and beers are twisted open as I tell the story of how the ocean nearly ate the Chook Chaser when it got stuck on the beach. As I speak the couple's attention wavers between me and the massive TV that dominates the room and on which, it appears, they are downloading every movie that's been made in the last ten years. Proudly they announce that through the internet on their phones, for only two dollars a day, they can download as much as they want.

The pair watch the graphs of downloading and uploading speeds intently. As a result the intelligence level of the conversation steadily drops. It's a strange situation I've gotten into and I can't help wondering, as I sip my beer, what the point of this so-called connectivity is if it hinders you from connecting with a real person who's sitting right in front of you.

Just as the company of a book in the tent starts to look good, the girlfriend's father walks in. 'My friend turned her car upside down and it's full of plants,' he says. 'I need to help her before the cops arrive.'

From the urgency in his voice I suspect what sort of plants they are as he grabs the car keys and rushes out the door. It isn't entirely clear to me what's going on, but due to the raised level of excitement I decide to stay a little longer. We have another beer and swap the downloading graphs for a downloaded Viking series with lots of violence and sex. Halfway through the second episode, the father returns.

I'm about to ask if his friend is OK when suddenly my jaw drops open. Standing in the doorway is this man in his fifties with at least ten weed plants in his hands. Not only that, but, 'There's more in the car,' he says, 'and we need to find a place for them.'

'Not in my house,' the daughter says, adamant. 'Take those things somewhere else before the cops get here. We've been in enough trouble before!'

They get into a serious argument about where to hide a carload of marijuana. Which I take as my cue to leave the scene.

The next morning I pass by the house. My new friends have promised to give me directions to a beautiful beach nearby. The issue with the weed plants must have been solved, as there is no trace of the greenery or the father. With the route marked out on the map, and a week's worth of food supplies, they send me on my way for my few last days of riding. As I mount my bike I go over the previous night's events. I still can't quite believe the scene that played out in the house of these rather ordinary-looking and friendly people. Well, I guess we all have a few skeletons we'd rather keep in the closet.

Chapter 9

Sunny Side Up

Life on the Sunshine Coast is pretty darn good. Writing articles based on my thesis and teaching at the university in Brisbane are not only great ways to stay busy and earn a bit of cash. I also genuinely enjoy doing them. On top of this, I couldn't have wished for a better place to work, or a better group of people to be surrounded by. The university is situated on the north side of Brisbane, so ideal for commuting. The buildings are new, the labs high tech and there is even a pool we can use for free. I'm fortunate to teach several classes to curious and inquisitive students. Of course, there is always the odd one out who needs to be put back in line every now and again, but I see this as part of the challenge, as well as winning the students' curiosity and motivating them to understand concepts they have never faced before.

The university staff is comprised of a young and enthusiastic bunch of Australians, English and a surprising number of Dutch people. One of them, Lisette, almost instantly becomes one of my closest friends. Four days a week I ride my two-wheeled steed a hundred kilometres back and forth to work, watching the sun rise over the sea in the morning and set over the mountains at night while zipping through bumper-to-bumper traffic.

My hunt for a house turns out to be another perfect, love-at-first-sight match. When Lisa and I meet we become so carried away in our conversation that she almost forgets to show me the house. We might have been cousins, or sisters even. Like me, she is short, physically active, blond, tanned and toned. Only Lisa's hair is a cascade of curls whereas mine is short and straight. I have to wait for her current housemate, James, to move out, but this feels like a formality. We are already talking about the trips we will do on the bike and the future surf sessions we'll undertake together at the nearby beach.

Within a week of moving to the Sunny Coast I find a perfect 7'4" surfboard at the same garage sale where Lisa buys a helmet. Surfing quickly becomes a big part of my life. On Saturday mornings we put the boards in the van, go to the beach for yoga sessions and afterwards continue the exercise in the water. Chasing waves is the perfect way to relax after my week at work.

I've also fallen in love with the house. Not only is it a mere five-minute walk from the beach. It is also full of air and light, with two bedrooms, a garden at the back and an open kitchen and living room with a balcony overlooking the street. White curtains hang over the sliding doors. The curtains move in the breeze which comes off the sea and tinkles the wind chimes on the balcony. Our shower always has sand in it, while bikinis hang drying over the screen. Lisa and I like to dance around the house in our underwear.

Arriving home late on weekdays I often open the door to the most amazing smells coming from the kitchen. Both Lisa and I are absolute food addicts. We love to cook. It's another thing we have in common. Shopping for food is a shared passion, which we indulge in every weekend, as is fantasising about the dinners we will create during the week. Although we are both petite, we constantly marvel at the rate at which we empty our lovingly stocked fridge. Beach life here with Lisa is every bit as awesome as I imagined it would be.

Easter Sunday is like every Sunday. I start with a run on the beach, then Lisa and I visit the local market and stock up on fruit and vegetables. Later we go surfing and afterwards lie about with our books, whiling the afternoon away. As night comes on, Lisa announces that she might go to a street festival. It turns out that

James has invited her, but she isn't sure if she feels like it. Free live music and a wealth of international food will make me move my ass from the couch any day of the year. I therefore convince Lisa to go and invite myself in the process. We are in absolute chill mode and reluctant to get all dressy. I wear a top over my sports bra and some heeled ankle-boots and cut-off jeans. Two minutes later we're in James's fancy car tootling down the road.

Both the food and the music are good, but as sometimes happens at such events, we lose track of each other in the crowd. I listen to the band, dancing along. Then when the band finishes and people move to the bars I spot Lisa, James and an unknown man a little further down the street. The stranger introduces himself as Mike, James's colleague at work. He's dressed in board shorts, a T-shirt with the image of a half-naked girl on it and a hat. He totally matches Lisa's and my straight-off-the-beach look.

While the other two head out for a cigarette, Mike and I remain at the bar. He starts the obligatory let's-get-to-know-each-other conversation. 'So what do you do?' he says.

'Well, at the moment I teach at university in Brisbane,' I reply, 'but actually I'm riding my motorbike around Australia.'

He looks at me, tilting his head slightly, and two seconds later he strings together the words, 'I think I'm a little bit in love with you.'

I'm intrigued by this sudden confession, before deciding that it's probably the alcohol talking, not to mention the cheesiest pickup line in the world. After James and Lisa return the four of us join a larger group and have another drink. There, from the corner of my eye, I see Mike making moves on Lisa, which reaffirms my suspicions about his come-on.

By the time the clock nears closing time, James's blood alcohol level is at least four times the legal limit. Instead of driving home, therefore, we decide to continue the festivities at Mike's house, which is just around the corner. Lisa and James both manifest themselves as quite the guitar players, while Mike and I take on the bartending job. We bring out red wine and whisky and the four of us go and sit down at the jetty outside.

Under the stars, by the light of the moon, we do our best Red Hot Chili Peppers and Beatles imitations. Then Mike and I have a long and heated discussion about attraction and choosing a partner. At this point, he isn't even trying to veil his whisky-inspired advances. I'm not particularly into him, but there is something about him that makes me curious. Usually, when I talk to guys, it gets boring within the first hour. I get the impression that my pigheaded, determined personality will steamroll right over them. But here is this stranger with a half-naked girl on his T-shirt, arguing that women make decisions with their reproductive organs more than men do, and I sense a welcome resistance.

Mike refuses to agree with my arguments. Somehow he counters every word I say and, amazingly, most of his statements actually make sense. There is no way he will allow me to perform my usual shock-and-awe flirting technique which goes along the lines of, 'I'm riding a motorbike around this country, can pitch a tent, make a fire and usually carry a pocket knife. I'm a badass and I can take care of myself.' In short, he is that rare breed I can get into the figurative flirtation boxing ring with and not necessarily expect to win. As Calvin Candie says in Quentin Tarantino's Django Unchained: 'I was curious before, but now you have my attention.'

However it's now four in the morning and one of the neighbours finally gets fed up with our drunken discussions and rock band imitations. He yells at us to go to bed, and, our eyelids heavy from red wine and whisky, this seems like a rather good idea.

Next morning James and Lisa want to leave early, but I'm too hungover to be upright and Mike displays a similar affection for his pillow. He says he can drop me home later, but 'later' turns into going out for breakfast, which turns into spending the day talking on the beach, which turns into having dinner together at my house. By the time he goes home I'm well and truly into him. I'm so into him that I get all nervous when we exchange phone numbers. I actually manage to forget his name, resulting in me handing over my phone and vaguely instructing him to put his full name and number in there while hoping the earth will open up and swallow me whole, trembling knees and all. A few days later he asks me out for dinner.

Over the next two months we spend most of our free time together. The idea that I will be leaving soon makes things less complicated than they would normally be. We can just enjoy the moment, no need to worry about the future. We go on hikes, go camping, have dinner dates and go surfing together. Even grocery shopping becomes a celebrated activity. We go fishing with his mum and I meet some of his friends. There's no weight in things that are usually labelled as massive relationship definers because I'll be leaving anyway. With the conversations we have, and Mike's view on life, he engages and inspires me. He totally turns my world upside down. No moment we spend together is boring.

Between being a full-time resident of cloud nine, working at university, riding my bike and cooking great dinners with Lisa, time flies by. Soon planning the next leg of my journey takes priority. After many lunchtime conversations, Lisette and I have decided to cross the desert together, going from Brisbane to Alice Springs, and from Alice Springs to Perth. She has a conference to attend in the Western Australian capital and venturing through the desert to get there seems more fun than taking a plane. But before we hit the dirt roads of the Australian outback, the Chook Chaser's luggage system needs a serious upgrade.

Walking over to Lisette's desk one day, the plan comes together in my head. The only luggage rack I can find that is desert proof needs to be ordered from the US. The costs of this trans-Pacific transaction can only be justified if this set of steel pipes will serve a journey lengthier than the crossing of a single desert. It becomes clear to me that somewhere along the line I have subconsciously decided that next year, after I've finished with Australia, my travels will continue in Asia with my beloved Chook Chaser.

'Lisette,' I say, 'getting the rack shipped here will take three weeks. That should give us almost three weeks to reach Perth. Do you think that's long enough?'

We look at Google maps, consider the number of non-sealed roads we will encounter, watch some videos on YouTube and come to the rather Australian conclusion that she'll be right!

Over the next weeks I eagerly await emails from various US postal services, cursing the unworkable seventeen-hour time difference between here and there while trying to communicate with the company that distributes these racks. It turns out that the package could not be sent through normal mail. As a result the shipping company has sent it back. Unfortunately, no-one bothered to enlighten me about these undesirable events and, after being returned, the rack has been sitting idle in the store's warehouse for almost a week. With less than a week to go before our planned departure there seems to be no other option than getting it shipped faster for a much higher price, crossing my fingers it will arrive within the necessary time frame.

On Wednesday, four days after D-day, the track-and-trace code reveals the long-awaited parts have finally touched ground in Australia. From this point the US tracing service stops so all I can do is wait anxiously for the desired box to arrive. Meanwhile, I sort through the closet full of belongings that I have acquired over the last two years. The arrival of this rack isn't just the arrival of a bike part. It also marks the end of my university life and the start of a journey that will take me to places I can't even imagine yet. Needing to lighten the load, therefore, I sort, box, discard and donate almost everything I've accumulated in Australia and even trade my dear surfboard in for two weeks of rent.

While I'm going through the last of my belongings, I hear the sound of a van stopping in front of the house and a door sliding open grabs my attention. I run down the stairs and there it is – forty by fifty by sixty centimetres of brown cardboard containing the foundations of my new foldable bedroom, bathroom, study and kitchen. The foundations of a new life, in other words.

Full of excitement and confidence I begin fixing the new metal frame on the Chook Chaser. All goes well until the wires of the indicators have to be extended. I graduated from spanners & screwdrivers primary school, a bit of oil is no issue, but as soon as I have to deal with electrics I'm back in kindergarten. In one hand I hold a bunch of electrical wires and little red plastic tubes that I assume to be the connectors. In the other hand is a completely useless manual, the type that makes instructions from Ikea look like the Encyclopedia Britannica. After an hour of doubtful pulling at rubber casings in a failed attempt to get to the wires where they enter the indicators, I opt for Plan

B: the good folk at the Yamaha shop.

Only a few days before these people replaced my chain, sprockets and rear tyre. I was allowed in the workshop, to learn how to do this in case of an emergency on the road. They laugh when I arrive back on their doorstep with a half-mounted rack and a backpack full of tools and sheepishly ask for their help. Once again they appoint me a spot at the rear of the shop.

'So you need a hand, do you?' Wayne, the mechanic asks.

'Yes,' I say, holding up the extra pieces of wire and the connectors that came with the rack. 'I have no idea where and how to extend the indicator wires.'

'Ah, that's easy,' he says. 'Come here and I'll show you.'

I watch intently while he cuts the first wire at the battery, under the seat, and then, with two connectors and a new piece of wire, extends it from there. I would have never dared to do this without his advice.

'Alright, girlie, think you can do the others now?' Wayne says as he hands me the tools.

She'll be right!

I get to work on the other wires, then reposition the indicators on the rack, tighten the nuts and bolts and connect everything up. Now and then as I work away one of the mechanics walks over to see how I'm getting on. And before I test the results, Wayne performs a thorough check.

To my delight, my handiwork passes with flying colours. By closing time everything's done and dusted and once again I pay my bill with a six-pack of beer. I then roll out the door, waving happily, while my latest teachers shout their goodbyes, wishing me a great journey across the red heart of Australia.

There are only two things left to do before setting off; arrange the luggage system and spending as much time as possible with the man I've fallen so hopelessly in love with. I manage to combine the two, with Mike helping me hunt down old suitcases and trawl through hardware stores for the necessary fittings. It is late on a Friday night when we step back and admire our work: two trolley bags, zip-tied on as panniers, and the plastic toolbox serving again as top box. Amazingly, it is all exactly as I imagined and designed it. Budget bike travelling has made us into true MacGyvers.

Next morning I pack what is left of my belongings. I have, eyes wide open, fallen into a trap I will later get to know as 'the danger of over preparation'.

Everything is ready for the desert, still over a thousand kilometres away, including ten litres of water and eight litres of spare fuel. The poor Chook Chaser is heavier than ever and my mood is not much lighter.

This is the first time in my life I will leave a place crying. The Sunshine Coast, although I've only lived here for four months, feels like home. Here for the first time I've lived in a way that I've been truly excited and happy about. If all goes well, Lisette and I will be back in Brisbane in two months to work for a few weeks. But in my mind, I'm closing this chapter and it's tearing me apart. It barely helps that I know I'm on the threshold of a journey that will change my life forever.

Then, to aggravate my struggle, there is this man. Mike treats me like a princess and gives more than I could ever dream of. Yet he supports my decision to leave, happily spending his free time helping to get the bike ready. We both know the connection between us is so strong that we will undoubtedly see each other again. But it feels wrong to ask him to sit around and wait for me. Looking into the clear blue eyes of the man who's turned my world upside down, I recognise the ridiculous dilemma of travel: leaving the certainty of a happy and comfortable life for the uncertainty of adventure.

I believe that when you really love someone you can't claim them or limit them in what they are allowed to do. For by imposing limits on someone you change who they are, until they are no longer the person you fell in love with originally. After avoiding it for as long as possible, a week before departure I finally woman up to the conversation we have to have and manoeuvre Mike out of the house. As we walk outside some rubbish bins across the street catch my eye. It's a shitty scenery for a shitty conversation, it actually fits the situation.

Always when playing out the scenario in my head I've been this confident woman, convinced of her beliefs and not afraid to express her thoughts. In real life, typically, I stutter my way through the carefully rehearsed lines.

'You know... I'm leaving and uh... Well, since I'm not here... And you have, you know, biological needs... So uh... If you want to see other girls... that's... that's OK...'

As soon as I finish the sentence it feels as if the weight of my entire luggage is lifted off my shoulders. Meanwhile, a look of surprise, with a hint of disbelief, appears on Mike's face.

Chapter 10

Desolate Deserts and Dust

Often, when people say they travelled through the middle of Australia, they're talking about the smooth strip of tarmac road that runs from Adelaide to Darwin. Lisette and I, however, take the less-well-beaten track from Brisbane to Perth through Alice Springs. On this route there are not only fewer people. There are also fewer fuel stations, fewer roads, especially sealed roads, and fewer signs of life.

With naive excitement, we both prepare for the day of departure. We listen to well-meant advice, about how dangerous the outback of Australia can be, yet don't always take it aboard. Mostly they're third-hand stories, not to be taken seriously. The people who spread them would be classified as fear mongers by the experienced long-distance travellers I will meet later in my journey. We have worked out our route and our capacity for survival. We pack lots of water, spare fuel, plenty of food, a good set of tools, a map and an emergency locator beacon. Last but not least we pack a bag full of Dutch down-to-earthness and a suitcase with common sense.

Lisette will drive the blue Holden Jackeroo 4x4 that she bought three weeks before departure. It's her first car, which she quickly nicknamed 'Jack', and in my book she's a badass for it. The car has been converted into an all-terrain camper and comes complete with everything needed for a full-blown glamping experience: table, chairs, comfortable double mattress with Ikea tags, sheets, pillows, plates, spoons, cups, even salt and pepper. Before we take off, Lisette receives a quick lesson on driving the vehicle and we plunder the Super Cheap Auto for spares and jerry cans and other bits and pieces. Later we rampage through the local ALDI collecting a week's worth of food. We're as ready as we'll ever be.

Lisette is waiting for me in Brisbane. When she sees me arrive on the contraption that used to be my motorbike her eyes nearly pop out of her head.

'Are you OK like that?' she asks, then, 'What *have* you done to your bike?'

She has never seen the Chook Chaser in full travel mode before, let alone in readiness for the Australian desert. We have silently agreed that we and our vehicles should be fully self-sufficient. I think it's part of the independent nature we share to do things this way. I assure Lisette both I and my overloaded bike are fine. We look at each other, eyes glistening in anticipation, but with one last hurdle playing on our minds: getting out of the city.

Lacking the 21st-century navigational option we have decided to go without – due both to cost and the conviction that we won't need it – we face a task that we will later rate as the second-toughest challenge of our entire trip. It almost follows therefore that while navigating our way out of Brisbane we have our first near-accident. It's a fairly typical scenario. Preoccupied with scouting for road signs, bamboozled by the maze of suburban streets, we miss the red light until we are right underneath it. We both slam on the brakes. Lisette's tyres screech and with a skidding rear wheel I only just manage to avoid Jack's tail-light. Everyone's told us the outback is dangerous, but what about the city. It's enough to make me wonder what we have gotten ourselves into.

Yet eventually we leave the madness behind and proceed just past Toowoomba, where we camp at the local showground. Lisette has never really camped before, so to have an actual toilet and even a shower nearby makes the transition to nomadic life a little easier for her. The second day we continue past Roma and slowly but surely distance ourselves from what is commonly known as civilisation. The towns become more widespread, the roads narrower and the kangaroos more plentiful. The early appearance of these unpredictable creatures forces us off the road in the late afternoon, after we decide it's too risky to continue. We follow a set of tyre tracks that veers off the main road, into the scrub, and discover a perfect camp spot. It is an open grassy area next to a seemingly unused train line which we call home for the night.

The next day we confront our first two hundred kilometres of gravel. Now the adventure is really on. We start off driving really slow, but I soon get the hang of it again, and Lisette and Jack follow swiftly. As the day unfolds we make the gravel home. Literally. We even camp between two massive piles of the stuff, watching from the comfort of our foldable chairs our first amazing outback sunset before lighting a small fire to stay warm. We're within view of the road and a little anxious someone might pass by. We're not sure we're allowed to spend the night on our little patch of gravel. Yet in the end we stay fifteen hours and in that time only a single road train, its three trailers brightly illuminated, passes by. At last we're off the beaten track, on our own. As we watch the flames we smilingly remember all the well-meant advice we were offered.

'Ow, such a hard life we have!' Lisette exclaims, laughing with sarcasm.

This is indeed the freedom we are looking for. But there are also a couple of dots on the map to aim for: first Alice Springs for the Finke Desert Race and, ultimately, Perth. And a time frame of just two short weeks to get there.

Every day we travel as far as we can. After starting out around nine each morning, the wheels keep spinning until the kangaroos come out to play at dusk. That night and the following morning are cold. The thermometer when we awake reads a meagre eight degrees. After watching the sun rise through the fogged-up rear window of the car, we reluctantly crawl out of our warm comfortable beds and prepare to start the day.

Unlike me, Lisette doesn't seem to be bothered by the cold. She's up and about, the kettle boiled and tea in hand, by the time I'm finally dressed. I wear leggings under my bike pants and stand about shivering and eating breakfast while Lisette is perfectly fine in her shorts. We joke about the irony of her being able to spend the morning driving in the warmth of her car, while I will do my very best not to lose a finger to frostbite. I knew the nights would be cold, but stupidly

She'll be right!

I didn't anticipate it would be freezing when we set off in the mornings. Three days into the trip I am faced with the shivering truth. There's nothing I can do about it except press on.

We pack the table, chairs and gas cooker safely into the car and I gear up to go. The sun is now well above the horizon, but the landscape is still draped in a beautiful, mysterious, silent early morning glow. After the first hour of riding, we stop to fill up the tanks at a service station. The small building serves as the heart of an eight-house outback village where two gravel roads intersect at a perfect right angle. I kneel down next to the bike. With my hands inside thin summer gloves, I grasp the engine and feel the life return to my fingers. Sitting there on my knees I fully realise that despite the slight discomfort, there isn't a place in the world I would rather be. The previous night's campfire conversation comes back to me. These coming weeks, life will be utterly simple but endlessly beautiful. The obligations and the busyness of the city are behind us. Ahead lies kilometre after kilometre of stunning emptiness. All we have to do is keep moving west, survive and enjoy.

Not long after leaving the service station I become overconfident on the gravel. While looking at the beautiful nothingness around me, and a kangaroo far away in a field, I fail to slow down enough on a bend.

The rear wheel hits some banked-up gravel, and the bike starts sliding. I try to correct things, but only manage to send the bike over the other way. I throw the handlebars over again in an attempt to keep upright. But before I'm properly aware of what is happening, I'm on my right side sliding along the road. Gravel hits my goggles. Instinctively I tilt my head away from the ground. Eventually I come to a stop and, still holding the bike, register what's happened. It's my first serious fall and it happened so quickly. I do a quick check of body parts. Surprisingly, nothing is causing excruciating pain.

Lisette kneels down beside me. 'Are you OK?' she asks, obviously concerned.

'Yes, I'm fine,' I say, 'but what about the bike? Is the bike OK?'

I'm still clinging to it, lying curled up in a sort of foetal position, fingers clenched around the handlebars, thighs gripping the seat. 'Can you lift it off me,' I say.

Somehow Lisette manages to raise the bike and I climb gingerly to my feet. I notice that the right pannier has been ripped off, while the rack seems to have protected my leg from serious damage.

She'll be right!

'Is the bike OK?' I repeat, seriously concerned about the Chook Chaser's well-being.

Lisette however is obviously, and rightfully, more worried about me than the bike. She puts me in a chair on the side of the road to recover. Later I will hardly remember much about this at all – clearly I was in a state of shock. Lisette will tell me that I sat there for at least half an hour, blankly staring ahead.

In my recollection, it's only a matter of minutes before there is a familiar noise. The sound of salvation. Motorbikes, many of them. *Bikers, here, on this deserted road?* It seems incredible, but there they are, fellow riders, right when we most need them. The feeling is like how you imagine finding an oasis in a desert just as you're about to die of dehydration. Most important of all, there's someone to check the Chook Chaser. Despite loud protest from Lisette, I rise from my chair and flag them down.

One by one six men arrive, pulling up and hopping off their two-wheelers. Like us, they are travelling to Alice Springs for the Finke Desert Race. Fortunately one of the men is a mechanic. After a quick but thorough examination he diagnoses scratches on the fender and headlight, a slightly bent rack and a right-hand mirror that's so badly scratched it's useless. In other words, the bike is now properly baptised and we're good to go again.

Still a bit shaky, I get back on my loyal steed. It's true what they say about climbing straight back on to the horse that's thrown you. Getting back on the bike is the only way I know to overcome my fears. Lisette has taken some of the luggage and put it in the car. The difference in the way the Chook Chaser handles is immediately obvious. Even so, the accident has shaken me and several times throughout the day I feel my heart skip a beat each time the rear wheel slides a fraction. It's a great comfort, therefore, to know that Lisette is right behind me. I can't quite imagine how it would have been if I were here on my own.

We continue riding until we reach Boulia at sunset. It's a deliberate push to make it this far, which will allow us to reach Alice Springs in time for the race. In the last kilometres, the sun hovers just above the horizon and shines through the trees lining the road. The light flickers among the leaves as visibility decreases. As always the threat of kangaroos is at the back of my mind, yet I have a comforting sense of certainty that we have dealt with enough for one day and that everything will be fine.

We enter the town just as the sun dips below the horizon, while woolly clouds blush candyfloss pink. The campground we pull up at has an actual toilet and shower. We welcome these luxuries with open arms after four days of wild camping and a slide in the gravel. After experiencing the glorious invention that is hot water coming from a source above your head, we cook nachos with a bean, corn, tomato and Mexican spice mixture and it's never tasted better. What a day and we're still in the outback. We haven't even hit the desert yet.

The next day we leave Boulia early, bound for Alice Springs. We take the Donohue and Plenty highways. Highway is a big word, though. In this part of Australia your backyard lawn could be a highway. Actually, it would be flatter, firmer and easier to ride on than the roads we find out here. Occasionally one will be well-graded, creating a smooth, clay-like surface. However most of the time loose gravel, potholes, corrugations and deep drifts of sand follow one another like beads on a necklace. The sameness of the landscape, meanwhile, accords well with our routine. We ride, we camp, we fill up our tanks at the occasional farm or local supplies shop. At night we sleep. Apart from the endless nothingness, the only view to please the eyes are the house-size anthills that rise out of the ground. After two days of this, literally shaken and rattled to bits by the constant holes and bumps, we reach tarmac again.

'It's only an hour to Alice Springs,' the lovely lady at

the roadhouse says. 'Just watch out for the cattle on the road.'

I inquire about kangaroos, but according to the lady they don't see many around here. So although dusk is setting in, we feel confident enough to complete the last stretch to Alice. Halfway through it I begin to wonder why it is so hard to see. As we slow down to avoid colliding with a cow I realise I'm still wearing my sunglasses. Oops. I change my eyewear and we arrive at the Stuart Highway to complete the last seventy kilometres to the famous town in the middle of Oz. As always, I'm in front, with Lisette and Jack following closely behind. It is getting really dark now, but with the amount of traffic on the road we're sure no kangaroos would dare to jump across it. We'll be fine.

All the way to Alice there's a comforting set of headlights in the mirror. We are overtaken by other cars every once in a while but I am convinced the two white lights in the mirror are Jack's piercing eyes. Arriving in Alice Springs I pull off the road so we can discuss where to find a campsite. Surprisingly, Lisette and Jack are nowhere to be seen. *What's happened? Is everything OK?* In the dark and unfamiliar town, exhausted after miles of brain-shaking gravel, my imagination goes wild. Five minutes later I'm convinced that Lisette must have had a terrible accident. *What was I thinking, pushing on through in the dark?* Just when I'm sure I'm about to go mad, Lisette pulls up beside me.

'I can't see a thing,' she says, pointing at the dashboard.

Her dashboard lights have given up on her. Most likely, the thousand kilometres of nineteenth-century highway got the better of one of the connections. Now she's flying blind, unable to see any of the dials.

The reason we've raced to Alice tonight is to attend the scrutineering for the Finke Desert Race. In this well-known event motorbikes, buggies and cars race hundreds of kilometres through the sand from Alice Springs to Finke township and back again the next day. On Friday night, when we arrive, all the competitors gather to have their vehicles inspected and show them off to the public. It is a heaven for bike enthusiasts and petrol heads. There are motorbikes everywhere. About six hundred will compete in the race.

One bike, in particular, is getting a lot of attention. Most specimens on show are motocross bikes, or at least road trail bikes. But this beauty is a full-blown KTM factory rally bike, Dakar-style, but with luggage racks attached to it. Unfortunately there is no-one around to explain its unlikely appearance here in the middle of Australia. The only clue as to its rider are the stickers stating Lyndon Poskitt Racing and a Great Britain licence plate. Fascinated though I am, I can't put the puzzle together yet.

While I'm drooling all over two-wheeler heaven, Lisette stays with Jack and the Chook Chaser. The drive has worn her out and her blood-petrol content is a bit lower than mine anyway. When I finally arrive back, I can see something is wrong. The car looks fine, and the bike is just as dusty as I left it, but Lisette's facial expression predicts bad weather. She quickly informs me, 'Some kids tried to sit on your bike.'

'Really?'

'When I told them not to, they ignored me. And then when I insisted they turned against me, yelling all sorts of insults and throwing rocks at me before running away.'

She looks forlorn, poor thing, but at least she isn't hurt. 'Thank you for protecting my bike,' I say, touched by her loyalty.

It's been a long day, so we decide to find a campsite and eat some nourishing food. On the way out of town we encounter a traffic jam. The two-lane roads can't cope with the influx of visitors for the race. We also discover, when we see flashing blue lights, that the police have set up a checkpoint. When we pass through it I notice a policeman shine a torch into Lisette's car. I know she must be worried about her malfunctioning dashboard. Stuff like that could get her a hefty fine. Fortunately the policemen fail to notice the problem and later we learn that they weren't looking for traffic infringements anyway. It turns out some criminals have escaped from the local prison and the police are pretty eager to find them again.

We park between some other travellers at a dusty spot just out of town. Exhausted from the challenging day we quickly put our heads on our pillows. Even the notion that stone-throwing kids and escaped criminals could be roaming around right next to us doesn't prevent us falling into a deep sleep.

Next day we go to the prologue. Dust and exhaust fumes fill the air. There's a constant buzz and hum of voices as we make our way through the crowd. We have arranged to meet Scotty, my mate from Bribie Island. One of his friends has flown over from England to participate in the race. Once we find them we are introduced to Eddie and Lyndon. After exchanging the usual formalities, Lyndon explains that he has ridden the big Dakar bike, also known as 'Basil', all the way from England to participate at this meeting in the middle of Australia.

At first I think he is joking, but then, noting his accent, I realise he's telling the truth. When he sees the confusion on my face he reassures us that this really is what he is doing.

'Damn, that's cool!' I say, knocked out at meeting this guy.

Later on we learn that he's pretty famous. He has his own series on YouTube called *Races to Places*, which shows his adventures as he travels around the world from one race to the next. I find it very inspiring.

We have a great day with Scotty, Eddie and Lyndon, but, unfortunately, we are on a tight schedule to make it to Perth. So the next morning we set off to see the sites around Alice Springs. We take the Mereenie Loop Road to see Kings Canyon and various other impressive gorges. At Yulara we acquire the necessary paperwork to travel on the Great Central Road and then finally make it to Uluru, or Ayers Rock. We're both blown away by how high this immense red rock towers up out of the flat country that surrounds it. Seriously, the thing is massive. As we are there late in the day, we watch the light of the sinking sun turn the red colour even more vibrant while the sky overhead is an intense blue with a few fluffy white clouds. It is stunning.

A few kilometres further on we embark upon the long-anticipated Great Central Road, where we quickly find a spot to call home for the night. A good meal and an early night should prepare us for the next leg of the adventure.

Chapter 11

Life Lessons while Looking Like a Racoon

The Great Central Road, which is 1,126 kilometres long, runs from Yulara in the middle of the Northern Territory to the mining town of Laverton in the southwest of Western Australia. All but a negligible few miles of this great track are unsealed. We've used our rest day in Alice Springs to stuff the car with food again. We've also showered at a petrol station on the way to Uluru and received some basic travel advice regarding the route from a few bearded bikers.

'Camp where no-one can see you', they say. 'Don't enter the communities and she'll be right!'

Lisette checks the oil level of the car, while I tighten the chain on the bike. 'Let's do this!' we tell each other.

She'll be right!

Once underway we continue our simple life. By day we put the kilometres behind us. Then at night we find a nice spot to camp. Every evening we marvel at the intensely colourful sunsets. Then, as the desert shadows gather around us, we cook ourselves a great big meal. When we brush our teeth, we spit white toothpaste on to red sand. Usually we read or watch the stars, before crawling into the comfort of the double bed in the back of the car.

We can't help remembering the people who warned us about the dangers of the desert. Yet here we are making memories for life. Our only true worry is working out how best to park Jack to watch the sunrise through our bedroom window. Finding good toilets in the outback also proves tricky. In no man's land, you don't have to worry about anyone leaving the seat up. It's more important to find a spot where the splashback on to your shoes or bike boots is minimal. In no time at all we identify our three major outback problems:

1. The Blue-Tack holding up the curtains in the car melts due to the heat.
2. When the corrugations are really bad, the windscreen wipers in the car turn themselves on.
3. The air-conditioning blows clouds of red dust right into Lisette's face.

Repeatedly encountering these challenges, we cry out

to each other, with smug grins, 'Life's hard, isn't it? Oh, so hard!'

Riding on the seemingly endless gravel, however, remains a mental and physical challenge. I'm constantly afraid of sliding and falling like I did before. My hands hurt from the shaking and my right arm and shoulder are locked in a constant throttle-open position. Every hour we stop and I self-medicate my arm and neck muscles back into functioning order with a large dose of tiger balm. On top of this, the riding makes me incredibly hungry. All the time. To divert my thoughts from these bodily issues I begin to think of riding on gravel roads as a metaphor for life. In my head I go through the lessons that this corrugated road is literally drilling into me.

Firstly, life is better when you travel on gravel. Yes, it might be more dangerous, but it is also more beautiful and far more rewarding. A gravel road forces you to slow down. This is something we should all do a bit more of in real life. Gravel is also off the beaten track. It takes you to places no other road goes. Few other people go there either. In short, gravel takes you to the most untouched and unspoilt places on earth.

The second thing I've realised is that gravel challenges you to rely on yourself, to trust your preparation and your skills. Plan ahead or plan to fail. It's not just a cliché. After riding over two thousand kilometres it has really sunk in. This is true of life in general, of course, not just of riding on gravel, but when you're doing seventy or eighty kilometres an hour on a potholed, corrugated track, you have to be constantly thinking of what lies ahead.

Finally, there's only one thing that's certain, and that is that everything will change. The credit for this wisdom goes to a greater philosopher than me. However it's a lesson I've really understood after covering many miles on outback highways. Imagine riding on an unsealed, but smooth and easy road. You look around to see the mountains, check for wildlife. Then, in the blink of an eye, you find yourself in the middle of loose rocks, sand, piled up gravel and other stuff that's tough to navigate. Yes, I'm sorry to say that sooner or later your nice smooth road is bound to change. The good news, however, is that it works the other way too. It's just a matter of pushing through, keeping the throttle open, and holding on until things turn back around.

All this thinking, plus the challenging road, totally occupy my attention. So I get a surprise when I glance into the mirror and the expected image isn't there. No Jack, no Lisette. I immediately pull up and wait a while before turning back. A kilometre or so down the road I see Jack parked to one side. Lisette is running around excitedly with her camera. She's pointing the lens to the right of the road. They are about a hundred metres away from us, camels, at least twenty of them. Luckily Lisette has been paying attention. With my eyes glued to the track I rode straight past them.

Now the real thing is finally here before us we click and zoom away like a couple of wildlife photographers on safari. When we finally decide we have enough footage to fill three photo albums we get in, and on, our respective vehicles and prepare to drive away. Yet before we've even started the engines, one by one the camels cross the road. Up close they are much bigger and more impressive than they look from afar.

The Great Central Road runs through traditional Aboriginal land. You need special permits to enter the area and there are certain codes of conduct travellers have to comply with. These include no alcohol, using only special non-sniff-able fuel, no taking photographs of Indigenous people and no entering the communities, plus a few other guidelines to ensure the privacy of Australia's original inhabitants. Before we left on the trip many people told us horror stories about Indigenous people trying to steal fuel, or breaking into cars looking for alcohol. As down-to-earth Dutchies, we've dismissed most of these tales as exaggerated or blown out of proportion. However we decide to stick to the rules and be extra careful. Just to be safe.

Aboriginal communities, and therefore fuel stops, lie about two hundred kilometres apart. With the three hundred kilometre fuel range of the Chook Chaser, skipping one is not an option. The first fuel station after Uluru is in the community of Docker River. According to our map, we should be approaching it. There are no signs but a small track leads off the main road. Lisette decides to check it out while I wait at the intersection.

When she's not back within five minutes, I go after her. The track curves to the left and leads towards a few houses. When I go closer I can't quite comprehend what I'm looking at. The houses are badly run down with windows missing and doors falling off their hinges. They are enclosed within metal fences over a metre high. The yards are filled with rubbish, broken toys, household appliances and cars with cracked windscreens or missing wheels. Stunned by the sight of this I slowly ride to the middle of town. Lisette is parked near a petrol pump contained within a metal cage that has a big lock on it. The expression on her face mirrors mine. As a dozen stray dogs surround us we look at each other, wondering where we crossed the border into a Third World country.

Inside the petrol station we are momentarily back in the Australia we know. The smell of deep-fried goods penetrates our nostrils. The store contains, apart from a window full of hot chips, some chocolate bars, one pear and two apples. A chubby, white, middle-aged guy with a typical outback accent approaches us. As he opens the gigantic lock on the petrol pump and fills our tanks he tells us about his experiences with the Indigenous locals. He has been here for years, he says, loves working here and wouldn't ever want to leave. 'Once you get to know them they are amazing people,' he adds.

At that moment a purple car pulls up behind us. The guy leans out the window, revving the engine and honking the horn at the same time. The windscreen is badly cracked, and a door is missing. I believe what the service station owner says about the Indigenous people being wonderful, but with this impatient, angry, revving and honking guy behind me, my threshold of discomfort is exceeded. I just want to pay the exorbitant $2.50 per litre of fuel and get the hell out of here.

For many bumpy kilometres, the images of the aboriginal community keep flashing before my eyes. We didn't know what to expect when we arrived, but this sure wasn't it. When it comes to the Indigenous, Australia's past will likely haunt the nation for many years to come. It is a topic little spoken about in everyday life or by mainstream politicians. In fact, I'm sure many of the nation's policy makers have never seen places like Docker River with their own eyes. Tony Abbott's recent remarks that living in an Indigenous community, on ancestral lands, is a 'lifestyle choice' not worthy of government funding, speaks clearly of the lack of knowledge and interest in the Indigenous people's ancient and uniquely rich culture.

The visit leaves both Lisette and I in a weird mood for the rest of the day. It is so clear that something is wrong and, as human beings, we want to help, but it's impossible to know exactly how.

Aggravating this confusion, the road is lined with cars that have been crashed and left there to rot. Some of them are still rather new. Others look ancient. I can't help wondering who was in these cars when they crashed. *Did they survive? Were they, as some would have you believe, 'high and drunk Abo's' who turned their cars over?* I was shocked the first time someone made a comment like this. Coming from overseas I've only ever been taught about the rich culture of the Indigenous and their close relationship with nature. Docker River, and what we saw there, is in direct conflict with everything I've learned. Nevertheless, I sharply resent the generalising, judging and racist remarks people make about the Indigenous.

On several occasions we are overtaken by vehicles that shouldn't be allowed on a normal road, let alone a treacherous strip of sandy gravel. We see five or more people packed into tiny sedans, most of them with the characteristic cracked windscreen. Sometimes the rear window is absent too. But, with the exception of one person, all the drivers wave when we wave at them and sometimes the kids press their noses against the window to get a better look at the bike.

The truth is, what goes on here in this beautiful and near deserted part of Australia lies far beyond our comprehension. Maybe that's why colleagues and friends, as well as random strangers, are so apprehensive about us being here. They don't understand this place and, as a result, are irrationally afraid of it. It doesn't help that you only hear about it when things go wrong.

As we proceed we learn that this is the only petrol pump located inside a community. So it is hard to judge whether Docker River is the exception or the rule. Every other time we fill up it is far away from the village. But most of the pumps also serve as the local minimart where we see plenty of Indigenous people. While the mums shop the barefooted kids can't stop laughing and pointing at me. At first I'm unable to figure out what they're carrying on about. Then Lisette points out that it might be my looks. When I look into a mirror I realise that I resemble an exotic descendent of the racoon family. Most of my face is covered in red dust, while the skin around my eyes, which has been protected by the goggles, is starkly white. The kids have the time of their lives and although I want to interact with them, play with them, something stops me.

To obtain permits to travel here we've signed a paper saying we wouldn't enter the communities and actively seek contact with Indigenous people. Back then the woman at the desk said it was all about letting people live their lives. Yet combined with all the scary stories we've heard, things like this create a mental barrier. Whereas the normal, human reaction would be to have fun with these kids, I hold back, torn between what I think is right and what I feel is right.

Long stretches of empty road only confuse my thinking. *Is it fear that keeps me from playing with innocent children?* It's obvious that both my view and behaviour have been heavily influenced by other people's opinions. I don't understand it and can't figure out the reasons behind my thoughts and actions. Eventually, after much inner turmoil, I come to believe that before Indigenous people can be successfully integrated into Australian society the people in that society must change their thinking about Aboriginals and approach them with different expectations. The sad truth, though, is that the problem is far too complex for me, and probably also the majority of Australians, to understand.

Yet regardless of the cultural shock we've received, life on the Great Central Road remains as simple and entertaining as ever. The jokes about how hard our life is continue. The outback 'problems' we face are just the same. As we travel further westward we become so comfortable with each other and our unpopulated surroundings that one day, sorting through her photographs, Lisette discovers me squatting and peeing in the background of one of her selfies. We laugh until our bellies hurt at finding this priceless display of exhibitionism.

One evening we camp at a spot with some freshwater springs. Footprints of camels and cattle surround these natural desert wells. We are amazed by this environment that is so foreign to us. We are in nature, part of nature, just the two of us here in the middle of the desert.

We eat dinner and are just getting ready for an early night when we hear a car approaching on the road. The corrugations function like a base speaker, carrying the sound of the approaching vehicle for kilometres through the silent darkness. Usually the sound comes closer, passes and then fades as the car disappears into the distance. Every time we hear the noise we turn off the lights, so as not to be seen. After a few days, this has become standard procedure. We hardly think about it anymore.

But this time around the car doesn't go past. 'Shit, no, no, no!' I say, as we listen to it slowly approach. All the scary stories we've heard of angry, high-on-petrol-fumes, Indigenous people looking for alcohol come back to us. All the news reports of backpackers being kidnapped and scenarios like in the Wolf Creek movie enter our thoughts. We're in the middle of our grooming ritual, baby-wipe bath and brushing teeth. Panicking, unable to think of anything better, I spit out the toothpaste and hiss at Lisette, 'Quick, get in the car.'

We grab our belongings and with our shoes on and our toothbrushes in our mouths jump in the car and dive under the covers. From behind the headrests of the seats in front of us, we peek at the car. Our heartbeats have sky-rocketed. We watch, with held breath, as the car drives around and then stops with its headlights pointing straight at us. The most unlikely scenarios play through my mind. *What if they use one of the chairs to smash in the window? What do we do if they want fuel or money? What if they have weapons?* The driver of the car then switches on its spotlight and the glare is blinding. We both realise that we are in the middle of nowhere. The closest village is a hundred kilometres away. Feeling defenceless and vulnerable, I think how stupid we've been to believe that it was all fine and dandy for two girls to cross the desert alone. *Why didn't we listen to all that well-meant advice?*

But suddenly the spotlight goes off and, moments later, the car turns around and drives away. *Phew*. We both breathe out in relief and Lisette gives a scared little laugh. When we come to our senses we conclude that the people in the car were campers, just like ourselves, checking out the spot. Still a bit shaky, but relieved, we open the doors of the car, take our toothbrushes out of our mouths and get into bed properly. With the adrenaline still rushing through our veins, we laugh at the memory of the shocked expression on each other's face when the car first arrived and the way we let our imaginations get the better of us until finally we fall asleep. Moments like these I'm so thankful I'm not alone.

Chapter 12

A Short Surprising Dip into Civilisation

At 4.30 a.m. the alarm goes off. Waking suddenly, I look out through the car window. It's still pitch black outside. I wonder why the alarm is going off while it's still dark. Then I look a bit closer and realise we're in a parking lot, not the middle of the desert.

We're in Kalgoorlie, the famous gold-mining town. Today our destination is Perth, the capital of Western Australia, still almost six hundred kilometres away. Up first as usual, Lisette opens the door and cold air fills our cosy little bedroom. Reluctantly I follow her lead, crawling out from under the blankets. By the time I'm dressed and back from the toilet, Lisette is already pouring the hot water into our cups.

It's cold, really cold, and I'm thankful to warm my hands on my tea while putting together our breakfast of fruit and oats. We eat quietly by the light of our head torches. Then we pack up the table, the gas cooker and the food. By 5.30 we are ready to go, only, against our expectations, it's still pitch black. I check my phone. The previous evening both Lisette and I contacted our families, to tell them that we're back in the land of the living. I also tried to call Mike, but he didn't pick up. When I call again this morning his phone is turned off. Strange.

Although it's still quite dark we decide to go. Riding the bike is far from fun this morning. Jack's thermometer reads ten degrees Celsius, and as we leave Kalgoorlie it starts to rain. I squeeze the handlebars and kick my feet on the pegs to keep the blood flowing through my extremities. After an hour I closely resemble an icicle, unable to feel my fingers in the wet gloves, and constantly shivering and shaking. The good news is that the rain has cleared. We have a short break at a small parking space beside the road. The scrub lining the pavement is littered with rubbish, a reliable sign of so-called civilisation. I leave my gloves on the hot engine, where they quickly dry, while I run around the parking lot to thaw my frozen body. The rest of the day remains grey and cold, but we manage to dodge the rain.

The roads are long, straight and mainly empty. However when we encounter a line of trucks I quickly lose sight of Lisette. We always travel slowly, one behind the other. The loaded bike sits comfortably at eighty. Anything faster conjures unpleasant noises from the engine and doubles the fuel consumption. When we are confronted with other cars they are often in a hurry to get past us. So too are the road trains that haunt these parts. It's tough when we get stuck between these monsters, the big trucks overtaking us on roads which have only one lane going each way. When they pass I have to hold on tight as the side winds they create push and pull the helpless little Chook Chaser all over the place.

When we stop for lunch Lisette immediately walks around to check her mirror. She looks pale. When I ask her what's wrong she tells me how one of the road trains cut her off. At eighty kilometres per hour he pushed her off the road on to the sandy shoulder and in the process scraped Jack's mirror. What made the incident worse was that he started overtaking on a hill and traffic popped over the hill just before he was fully past her. The damage to Jack is minimal, but it takes Lisette a while to shake the incident off.

The rest of the way to Perth is relatively boring, but luckily we complete it without any further issues. We pass a few sleepy towns dotted along the way. Our progress brings us not only closer to the Western Australian capital but also closer to the sea. In the late afternoon the clouds break open and golden sunlight spills down, illuminating the rain-washed land. The last few kilometres are really quite pleasant.

As soon as we arrive we search for Gert-Jan and our university colleagues who have come over for the conference. When at last we find the group, Gert-Jan enthusiastically drags us up in front of all the professors and PhD students who have gathered and says, 'So, tell us about your trip!'

Thirty pairs of eyes stare at us curiously.

'Uhhmm,' I start, trying to pull myself together. I look at Lisette for assistance, but she's just as lost as I am.

After travelling five thousand kilometres we find the moment overwhelming. The journey has changed us. An environment that we were perfectly familiar with, and comfortable in, only two weeks before now seems unutterably foreign and strange. Neither Lisette nor I have got our bearings yet or processed the journey. We were hoping for a more gradual re-entry into civilised company. We're also surprised to see everyone together like this, not having expected quite so many people to know about our trip. To make matters worse, I'm covered in red dust and my hair looks like a greasy crow's nest because we haven't showered in a week. Fortunately our audience is keen and patient with us, so that as we clumsily stand there, our story spills out.

She'll be right!

Afterwards Lisette and I manage a quick change of clothes, though the shower will have to wait. We then join our colleagues and, still feeling a bit stunned, walk to a nearby restaurant.

During the walk I have a few minutes to call Mike. I tell him we've made it to Perth safely and even survived a wildfire of questions from all these university types. I explain how confusing it's been, this cold-turkey return to university life.

'Right now we're running after three professors, heading for a restaurant.'

'Oh, that's a shame,' Mike replies. 'I was hoping to take you out for dinner.'

I don't know what sort of reply I was expecting, but this is a shock. I pause for a second, thinking that all that continuous riding might have damaged my hearing, before answering, 'Yeah, that's nice, but this isn't the moment for a Skype date.'

Mike laughs. 'No Skype date,' he says. 'I'm in Perth.'

'What!?! No, you're not...'

I send him directions, but still can't quite believe it. After two weeks of solitude, first the reception at the university and now this. Lisette, I need to talk to Lisette. As soon as I tell her she starts to laugh.

'That's exactly what I thought when he didn't answer his phone last night.'

Half an hour later Mike walks into the restaurant, all smug smiles, proud to have pulled off this massive surprise.

Chapter 13

Winding up a Wet West Coast

After an unforgettable weekend in Perth, Mike flies home and Lisette and I reunite. We commit to some household tasks, like washing the red sand out of the sheets, and prepare our vehicles to continue the journey north to Darwin. Our first stop is the famous Pinnacles Desert, in Nambung National Park.

Travelling north from Perth, the vast Indian Ocean on our left, we see clouds starting to build up. We manage to dodge the showers and after a handful of hours arrive at our destination. The Pinnacles are weird and amazing, a mass of ancient, naturally formed pillars of yellowish rock, ranging in height from a few centimetres to several metres, extending across an expanse of parched and rumpled sand. We wander among these mysterious outcrops in awe and that evening watch a beautiful sunset, the cloud-streaked sky to the west turning lilac and amber and rose. Our camp that night is the caravan park in the town of

Cervantes, where we have a nice shower, a solid meal and a good night's sleep before heading off into the wilderness again.

There are places Lisette wants to see in this region that I visited with my parents last year. I meanwhile have begun to miss travelling on my own, the thrill of the empty road and having to rely entirely on myself. Travelling solo is an addiction and I've become badly hooked after riding all those kilometres around the south and east coasts of Oz. Though being with Lisette has been fun, I need some time off to roam alone and attend to my own wants and needs.

When I suggest that we separate for a bit, Lisette immediately agrees. Both of us and our vehicles are entirely self-sufficient. Moreover, the plan has always been to cross the centre together and then see what happened afterwards. With a big hug we say our goodbyes, wish each other a safe trip and agree to meet up again in a week, before embarking upon the Gibb River Road.

Today there is no avoiding the rain. Several big downpours land right on my helmet and by midday I'm soaked. Towards the end of the day I look for a spot to spend the night. One of the things I love most about Australia is that there is always a place to camp. It is what people do, travel and camp, leaving nothing behind but the ashes of a small fire. I follow a well-worn track away from the road, into an open area where there are indeed the remains of camp fires. I go a little further into the scrub, away from the sound and lights of traffic, telling myself that this will do for the night.

Just then I strike trouble. My body is tense, negotiating the soft wet ground. Suddenly, influenced by whatever mysterious power controls these events, the front wheel hits a rock and starts to slide from under me. I put my feet down and try to hold the bike upright, but my boots fail to grip on the slippery red mud. The bike falls and I only just manage to avoid getting trapped underneath it.

I step back and look at the fully-loaded Chook Chaser lying on its side. Realising it will be much easier to lift without the luggage, I wrestle to untie the straps and remove the dry bag from the toppled-over bike. Unfortunately the panniers are zip-tied to the rack and hard to remove so I leave them on. I then gather all my force and attempt to lift the bike. Again the mud works against me. The front wheel slides away. I put some rocks around it to keep it in place. Finally with a last effort, pulling desperately, I manage to lift the Chook Chaser back on its feet. Fortunately the rain begins to ease and I quickly pitch the tent. Warm and dry in my nylon home I eat leftover pasta from yesterday. Then, exhausted as I am, I fall asleep with my face in my book.

Next morning the weather hasn't changed. During a rare dry spell I quickly pack up the tent and strap all my belongings on to the bike. A cold wind blows large grey clouds about. The rain pours down before I get the chance to escape the red clay. Carefully I navigate back to the road, not feeling like repeating last night's power-lifting exercises.

Back on the road my mood mirrors the sky. I don't have any protection from the rain. Riding in Kevlar jeans and a simple bike jacket isn't helpful. I bitterly regret throwing away some bright yellow rain pants before leaving the Sunshine Coast, even though they were ripped. Since the beginning I have done without wet weather gear, simply hoping that it wouldn't rain, and give or take the odd shower, mostly it hasn't. But today my luck has run out and I'm cursing my optimism. The cold water finds my skin and quickly sucks out what little warmth is left in my bones. This is the downside to motorbike journeys – being exposed so intimately to your surroundings, though a uniquely enticing way of travelling, can leave you vulnerable when the elements turn against you.

The road seems endless. The tarmac is a shade darker than the looming sky, and my mood a shade darker than the tarmac. Attempting to cheer myself up I think back to the weekend with Mike in Perth. I still can't quite believe he flew all that way just to surprise me. For a few minutes I'm on cloud nine, not feeling the rain or the cold, only the warmth of his imaginary arms around me. But soon enough my thoughts take a downturn until they once again match the inky black sky.

Things become worse when I start to imagine what will happen to us when I have to leave Australia. We aren't officially together. On the contrary, I have given him permission to see other girls. Yet at the thought of losing him it feels like a big fist grabs my heart, twists it ninety degrees and rips it out of my chest. This isn't me. Sure, I fall in love, everyone does. Maybe it's the impossible nature of the situation, the inevitable goodbye at the end, that makes it so special, so intense. Or maybe it's just my current physical and mental fatigue exaggerating my fears of leaving loved ones behind in search of a questionable life of adventure. Because right now, adventure has lost every bit of its glamour.

My dark thoughts are put to flight by the sight of a roadhouse ahead in the distance. I pull up outside and, soaked and shivering, peel my tense body off the bike. I fill the Chook Chaser up with petrol and treat myself to hot chips to warm up. Then, walking out of the warm comfort of the roadhouse, a familiar blue vehicle pulls up next to me and Lisette jumps out.

It's only been a day since we parted, but I'm really happy to see her.

'So where are you going now?' I ask her.

'First to Monkey Mia, then Exmouth and Karijini National Park,' Lisette replies. 'And you?'

'Same,' I say, staring into the distance.

I start to wish we were travelling together again, even though I'm aware that I was the one who suggested we part ways. The weather forecast is for more rain. And to be honest I feel like shit, both mentally and physically. On top of this the thought of sleeping in a wet tent again is a dismal prospect. Basically, I miss Lisette, her companionship and optimism and her caring nature. I also miss Jack's comfort.

When I timidly suggest that we continue together it feels like I'm asking forgiveness for wanting to go my own way. I'm relieved when Lisette agrees, unsure whether she can sense how I feel. It feels good to set out together again, bound for Monkey Mia further up the coast. My body is still cold and I ride curled over the handlebars to avoid the rain stinging my face, but

She'll be right!

with the comforting image of Lisette once again in the mirror, my mood warms up quickly.

Monkey Mia is famous for its dolphins. Wild dolphins have been coming here for years to be fed by volunteers. The dolphins appear regularly off the beach and you can see them playing about in the sea. We move into the campground, only a few hundred metres from the shore. A hot shower in the toilet block filled with steam brings my body temperature back to normal. A shelter provides a dry place to cook and eat. Halfway through the evening the rain graduates from on-and-off drizzle to a continuous downpour. It keeps raining all through the night. The next morning Jack stands like an island in a small lake, his wheels submerged in ten centimetres of water. Imagine being in a tent.

In the morning we join the tourists on the beach to watch the dolphin feedings. We stand in a group in the ocean with the water coming up to our knees. Every time a wave approaches, we jump up to protect our pants from the rising sea. People hold up a rainbow of coloured umbrellas to protect themselves, and their cameras, from the rain.

Somehow my fluorescent green hoodie stands out enough to get me picked from the crowd to feed Puck the dolphin. Excited like a little child I wade deeper into the water, holding the fish in my hand as this incredible mammal slowly glides by. When Puck takes the fish her head is tilted slightly, with one eye looking up at me, as if she wants to say thank you. She has no sooner captured her meal than she dives under the water and swims away, back out to sea.

Afterwards, I'm left nursing a warm inner glow. Regardless of whether you think it's a good or a bad thing to feed wild animals, it is easy to understand why people do it. It is magical to be so close to these kind and lovely creatures.

After Monkey Mia we set off to Exmouth and Ningaloo Reef. Excitedly we take our vehicles through a lot of water crossings. The rain has stopped falling but everywhere streams and rivers have overflowed their banks. In many places the water has found its way on to the road. Luckily here on the west coast all the roads are perfectly smooth tarmac highways. If this had been a dirt road, you could have opened a temporary mud spa on it. As we pass road signs sticking out of the middle of a river, warning us of 'Limited water supplies for the next 632 km', we conclude that this amount of rain must be extremely rare.

We leave the clouds behind as we come into Exmouth. It doesn't look too exciting but that doesn't matter,

She'll be right!

because just beyond the town lies Cape Range National Park. The main attraction here is Ningaloo Reef. I've looked forward to visiting this place ever since Andrew, the Scottish guy from Perth with the big BMW, so enthusiastically described it to me. Before plunging into the underwater world, we camp a night just outside the park. While we are cooking dinner, one of our neighbours comes over to say hello.

Sandra and her husband Ash are both in their seventies. Yet that doesn't stop them from exploring their country and towing their camper-trailer to its most beautiful and remote corners. Needless to say, they've got plenty of stories.

'One time we got stuck along the Birdsville Track,' says Ash. 'We thought we could make it through before the weather turned around.'

'But of course we didn't,' Sandra adds, laughing. 'A big storm took us by surprise and the entire track was washed out. We couldn't go anywhere for days.'

'What did you do?' asks Lisette. We're both captivated by the couple's adventurous spirit.

'We ate all our food, drank all our booze and had a great time,' laughs Ash. 'By the time we'd finished the road was OK again.'

We all burst out laughing. Time and time again I'm surprised by how the Aussies deal with seemingly catastrophic situations. Where other people would panic or go crazy, Australians sit down, have a beer and make the best of it.

'Yes, the worst situations always make for the best stories,' says Sandra with a wink.

We spend the entire evening with this remarkable couple. It feels like being at home in the Netherlands when grandpa and grandma share their stories of 'a long time ago when your mum was only a little girl...'

To explore the world and go on adventures like we are doing now, there are certain things you have to sacrifice. You can't be with your family when you're on the other side of the world. It's hard when you can't attend your grandmother's ninetieth birthday. I feel guilty that I have never met my brother's girlfriend, although he's been with her for two years already. You have to learn to live with these sacrifices. You also learn to appreciate so many small things, things you take for granted in everyday life.

Though it's only for one night, having this grandma and grandpa experience feels extremely valuable. Somehow it seems to bring us down to earth and make us realise what we've got. Next morning we bid Sandra and Ash a cheerful goodbye and, full of excitement, enter the national park.

It is too cold to jump in the water just yet. Exploring the park by foot first seems a better idea. On our walk, Lisette displays her excellent wildlife spotting skills again. She points to the other side of a small canyon. 'Look over there,' she says. 'That's a black-footed rock wallaby.'

It takes me another minute, and more directions, to get the creature in focus. 'To the left of that little bush,' says Lisette, pointing. 'Just up from the black dot, slightly right of those flowers.'

Finally I spot it. It's much smaller than the other wallabies I've seen. From this distance it looks like a little ball of fur with a long tail, tiny paws and pointy ears sticking out. Sadly, it's impossible to see from where we are whether its feet are black or not.

By midday both the temperature and the tide are perfect to walk off the long white beach into the wonders of the underwater world. That is exactly what Ningaloo Reef is, a stunning coral outcrop lying right off the beach. We use the mask and snorkel I've carried around the entire country just for this purpose and spend hours floating around on our bellies, our eyes fixed on the enchanting spectacle below us. The colours of the coral are amazing and we see fish with the most intricate patterns swimming about. The sand is pure white and the water a deep translucent blue. If you ask me, this is paradise right here. The sun is shining too, and it's warm, which makes our struggles with the rain and the cold a few days ago feel like they happened in a previous life. Truly, I would have liked to stay here forever. To me it's one of the highlights of our trip.

Because of my enthusiasm for sea life, we spend a little too long face-down in the water. Now Lisette wants to push on, as there are other things to do and see. We race through the supermarket, a little frantic, to stock up on groceries. Finally, while loading the groceries into Jack, the bomb bursts.

'We've got to hurry up if we want to make it to the canyon and find a spot to camp before dark,' Lisette says.

'I know, I know,' I reply. 'But I also have to call my parents and Mike before we head off into no man's land again.'

'Seriously, that too?' Lisette sounds irritated. 'We said we'd make it to Charles Knife Canyon.'

'I'm afraid we won't, Lisette,' I say timidly.

'It's supposedly even better than Kings Canyon,' she says, raising her voice slightly. 'I really want to see it.'

I feel guilty. It's my fault we stayed at the reef too long. I'm also the one who tends to take the most time over things. Lisette is a planner, while I tend to enjoy the moment. Sometimes I get lost in my own little world. There's also no way, once we're on the road, that the Chook Chaser can keep up with Jack. As a result of all this Lisette feels like she's missing out on things and that makes her unhappy, which is totally understandable.

'I'm sorry,' I say, looking down at the ground, not really sure what to do.

Lisette looks away, which makes me feel worse. Fixing the situation seems beyond my control.

'Do you want to split up again, travel at your own speed?' I reluctantly suggest.

It's not what I want. We both bring our strengths to the table and I'd really like us to finish the journey together according to plan.

'No, that's not it,' Lisette says, shaking her head, and

then falls quiet.

We're both hurt. By the time we finish packing the groceries we are more emotional than angry. I feel horrible. I don't want to ruin Lisette's trip with my 'seize the day' attitude. Yet I don't want to travel without her either. So we kiss and makeup.

'There's no-one else I'd want to do this trip with,' I confess, with tears in my eyes.

'Come here,' Lisette says and stretches out her arms. We seal our statements with a hug, hop in and on our respective vehicles and drive towards the sunset.

Slowly we make our way northward up through Western Australia. We leave the coast for a few days to visit Karijini National Park. On the way there we discover the advantage of the rain we've experienced, which is so rare in these parts. The road is flanked by gorgeous wildflowers. Millions of purple, white and yellow dots provide a stunning contrast with the red ground and rocks. For kilometre after kilometre we are enchanted by the simple beauty of nature.

The feeling continues when we visit Karijini, where over many years rivers have carved steep canyons into the red rocks. In a state of bliss we hike up and down cliffs, walk along rivers, swim in pools and shower under waterfalls. One of the waterfalls almost looks manmade. It is a wide wall of variously sized square-ish rocks, which sit one on top of the other and water flows down over them. Ferns and other green plants hang from the rocks and a kind of natural shelf protrudes from the wall, so that the water falls over it like a soft shower.

'That's how I want my bathroom to look when I have a house later on,' I say, pointing it out to Lisette.

Once we leave Karijini behind, we encounter long days of nothingness. We pass empty fields with only massive, weirdly shaped anthills to stimulate our imagination. We drive, eat, drive, set up camp, eat, sleep, eat, drive, eat, drive – all the way to Derby. Here we find the start of the famous Gibb River Road.

Chapter 14

Will We Make it?

The woman at the tourist information centre looks at us warily. 'We advise you to take at least two spare wheels,' she says, in a voice full of motherly concern.

Lisette and I look at each other, both thinking the same thought. The Chook Chaser only has two wheels. Jack has no space to put another spare wheel and we really can't imagine that we'll need more spare wheels than we've got. The woman means well and we nod thoughtfully, but we don't have the slightest intention of following her advice. We've only come to the tourist information to ask about the current road conditions and the water level in the Pentecost River. Unfortunately, despite her good intentions, the lady can't help us with either.

We therefore switch to Plan B. This involves stocking up on food, filling all the fuel tanks and asking elsewhere about road conditions. At the local roadhouse they are better informed and assure us that everything should be fine, although possibly, they say, the Pentecost might be a bit tricky.

There is every reason to be apprehensive. The Gibb River Road is regarded as one of Australia's most beautiful, yet toughest and most challenging roads. Yet by the sound of things the current conditions shouldn't stop us from taking it. We reason that if we can cross the desert we'll certainly make it out alive.

After lunch we set off for the infamous 660 kilometres of gravel. The Gibb River Road was originally constructed to transport cattle. It runs straight through the pure natural beauty of the rugged and lonely Kimberley region. During the wet season large parts of the route flood. Due to which the road is closed half of the year. The other six months tourists with sturdy 4x4s crisscross the largely uninhabited area.

It feels good to be underway and reach the gravel again. The last serious stretch was over two weeks before. I feel excited and also oddly comfortable. The feeling's a bit like returning to your own bed after a long holiday. There is no traffic, just anthills, pointing up like yellow-brown stalagmites, left and right of the road. As we trundle along all is just as it should be.

The first night we spend at Windjana Gorge where we

are treated to an incredible sunset and a cosy campfire session with some fellow travellers. One of the neighbours inspects the Chook Chaser and notices that its rear tyre is almost gone. I'm astounded. The idea of having to change a tyre before reaching Darwin has never occurred to me. Besides, this tyre has only been on for five weeks. The thousands of kilometres of gravel have shown no mercy. It has eaten away at the rubber at a serious pace. Luckily for me the same neighbour remembers that there is a tyre place not too far from where we're camped.

The next morning we are in no rush to get moving. This place is magical and we want to take in as much of its beauty as we can. Walking through the gorge we spot freshwater crocodiles sunbathing peacefully on the banks of the stream. They aren't dangerous, but this is the first time we've seen a crocodile in the wild and naturally there is excitement all over. Laughing like madwomen we pull out our cameras and click and zoom away at these prehistoric-looking creatures, observing their thick leathery skins and large exposed teeth. When we see other tourists take pictures of themselves with the animals, we become brave enough to do likewise.

Tunnel Creek is next on the list. As the name implies, it's a creek running through a tunnel that's rather like a cave. You can just walk in with a flashlight and wade

She'll be right!

through the water, which is basically what we do, in awe of the place's beauty and the epic grandeur of nature in these parts. Later that day we camp next to a river. While we cook dinner thousands of cockatoos fly from bank to bank against the backdrop of another spectacular sunset. Once again my jaw drops in wonder and gratitude.

On the road next day I have another magical experience. We leave early with the sun hanging like a glowing red ball just above the horizon. The landscape is empty apart from a few small anthills flanking the red dusty track. The track stretches all the way to the straight flat line where the red earth meets the deep blue sky before appearing to drop off the planet.

I'm riding quietly through this desert wonderland when suddenly, out of nowhere, a flock of cockatoos appears. The birds fly just in front of me, pure white creatures with a bright yellow hairdo, screeching their crazy laughter. They follow the bike for at least a kilometre. Then they disappear as suddenly as they came. Now I'm not a religious person, but it felt as if these birds were watching over me, welcoming Lisette and me to this stunning place and showing us the way. Telling us that everything will be just fine.

While I'm still mesmerized by the appearance of our flying friends, we are suddenly stopped in our tracks.

Smoke is rising from the scrub to our left. As we get closer we can even see flames. The temperature seems to rise and I begin to feel hot in my helmet and jacket. Concerned, we pull up by the roadside and try to work out whether the situation is dangerous or just some planned burning going on. Eventually we decide it's the latter, so like real tourists we take some photos and continue on our way.

We take a turn, off the main road, in search of a small waterfall. At first it's just another deep red track piercing the grassy emptiness. Soon, however, we discover that this route is something much more exciting: our initiation to real water crossings. In all honesty I have little clue about how to deal with these hurdles. The ten centimetres of water over the tarmac on the way to Exmouth was fun, easy, and harmless. But this is a proper creek we're facing, with a rocky bottom and murky brown water. I'm afraid that I'll drop the bike. If water enters the engine I would have no idea what to do. I can feel my heart beating in my throat, my heart rate doubled. But there is also positive excitement, the challenge of stretching our boundaries. *This is why we are here.*

We cross three creeks in a row, all of them quite shallow. But then the fourth creek we encounter dips much deeper than expected. You can't see what you're up for when you go in. So, as I've done the first three times, I put the bike in first gear, keep the throttle open and aim straight for the other side.

Halfway across, with the water reaching over the axles, I strike some big rocks and the bike starts to wobble. When I correct the first wobble I only worsen the situation. It then becomes a struggle to stay upright as a second big rock puts me on course for the high grass on the bank, which isn't good. I focus my efforts on reaching the road on the bank and just manage to make it, then catch the bike as it starts to drop. The front wheel is indeed in the high grass, leaving the rear wheel about a metre out of the water on the hard-packed red dirt.

Carefully I inch the Chook Chaser backwards, free the front wheel from the grip of the vegetation and ride on to the road again. Lisette is in the car, holding her breath as she watches this close call. Clearly I have to get better at water crossings before we attempt to make it through the dreaded Pentecost River.

At the end of the road we are rewarded for our efforts. There is an idyllic little waterfall, which we have all to ourselves. We relish the peace and quiet before retracing our steps. The creek crossings once again provide some good shots of adrenaline before we return to the main road.

Not much later we reach the tyre place mentioned by our neighbour two nights before. It's just a shack in the middle of nowhere. The guys there don't stock any motorcycle tyres but they are incredibly friendly. After inspecting the tyre one of them says, in a typical Australian way, 'She'll be right. That beauty will take you to the end of the Gibb.'

However, just in case it does go flat, they supply us with a set of extended instructions on how to fix it. And just to make sure we really know what to do, they repeat the routine once more.

With refreshed tyre-changing know-how and a healthy dose of optimism, we hit the road again, heading for Bell Gorge. Here we find a massive waterfall where we have our shower for the day. However in all its beauty this waterfall attracts too many tourists for our liking. Unfortunately, also, some of the tourists act like assholes. When we are standing at the top of the waterfall a guy tries to impress a bunch of girls by throwing a massive stone. It hits the rocks a few times on its way down, frightening the birds that fly off in all directions. Not willing to be part of this we clamber down to the water and jump in for a cleansing dip.

Lisette, with her wildlife-spotting talent, points out a lizard sunbathing on a ledge near the water. We watch this intriguing creature as he moves slowly to position his body optimally in the hot afternoon sun. Then the peaceful view is suddenly disrupted by a loud, overweight, ugly guy. Fully absorbed by his ego and his GoPro, he nearly crushes the sunbathing lizard in his attempt to take the perfect selfie. His actions display a type of disrespect I haven't seen much in Australia. True, there is some rubbish along the inland roads. But mostly I've noticed people care for their country and its natural beauty more than anywhere else in the world. Maybe these two men are an exception. Whatever the reason, when taking the best selfie gets the better of respecting the wildlife I find it sad and perplexing. We are soon out of there.

After all the warnings we've received and stories we've heard, we conclude that conditions here on the Gibb River Road aren't half as bad as we expected them to be. Travelling fast is definitely not an option, though, especially when we hit a stretch of road that bears a close resemblance to my primary school sand pit. Roads like this are all alike. No matter how deep you dig, there is more sand below. I stand up and move my weight to the back of the bike, making sure to keep the throttle open. Then, with tensed arms and a rear wheel that insists on regularly sliding, complete the thirty kilometres of sand pit. Soon afterwards we see two figures on the road, a pair of cyclists. *What an immense effort to cycle here,* I think, *on this surface in these boiling temperatures.*

Later the cyclists stop at the same camp spot and we spend the evening together. Their names are Luk and Sophie. They come from Belgium and are cycling from Perth to Darwin. We enjoy a great night together, sitting and talking beneath the stars. It's a pleasure to meet these courageous travellers.

Soon afterwards we approach the Pentecost River. Before attempting this tidal waterway, we stop at Home Valley Homestead to discover the best time to cross it. On the iron gate, written in beautiful, graceful lettering, is a poem.

We are all visitors
to this time, this place.
We are just passing through.
Our purpose here is to
observe, to learn, to grow...
and then we return home.
Aboriginal Proverb

As I read it I choke up. We open the gate, enter the property and park the vehicles. Lisette climbs out of the car and catches me staring into the distance with a puzzled look on my face. 'Are you OK?' she asks.

I attempt to say, 'Yes, I'm fine,' but fail miserably. Instead, tears well up in my eyes as the emotions of the past six weeks of travel catch up with me. I think of the immense physical challenge of crossing the desert, the long days spent with my thoughts in my helmet, the incredible natural beauty we've seen, the amazing sunrises, sunsets and starlit skies, Lisette's companionship, Mike's surprise visit to Perth, even working at university and living on the Sunshine Coast. The tumultuous waterfall of feelings sweeps over me, shaking me to my core but also confirming the sense I have of being where I'm supposed to be, doing what I'm supposed to be doing. The idea that I have to leave this country in less than two months haunts me.

'And then we return home'
But I am home! I want to scream. *I have never felt more at home than right here, right now, in Australia.*

Lisette puts an arm around me as I translate all this into words. She is the best friend I could wish for. After a few minutes I'm back to my normal self again and we continue on our mission. However, the feeling doesn't leave me.

We ask the girl at reception when low tide will be at the Pentecost River. She replies that it doesn't make much of a difference as the water only drops a few centimetres. We explain that, on a motorbike, a few centimetres can make a massive difference.

'Oh,' she says, 'but we only advise people to cross in a four-wheel drive.'

I want to counter that it is highly unlikely the Chook Chaser will grow a set of training wheels over the next few hours. However, in actual fact, I kindly stress the importance of knowing the tides, because I will be crossing on my bike. She repeats her advice to take four wheels at a time through the water before reluctantly checking the chart and telling us that low tide will be at 4.20 p.m. It is 1 p.m. now. Plenty of time for a relaxed lunch before setting off to the actual crossing.

After our favourite lunch of leftover pasta, we arrive at the crossing, park on the side to observe the situation and wait for the water level to drop. This is it. This is the hundred metres of rocky, boulder-strewn river crossing I have been both fearing and looking forward to for the past thousand kilometres. It is almost the end of the Gibb River Road. This means that if I and the Chook Chaser are unable to cross we will have to go back six hundred kilometres and detour another seven hundred to reach where we are going. When I see the first cars going through the water, carving a trail, all of a sudden turning around seems like a splendid idea.

With their wheels under water, these big 4x4s bounce

around on the boulders like little bubbleheads. But we didn't come all this way to just give up. The only way I wouldn't ride the bike across is if a truck appears and the driver offers to carry it to the other side for me.

Before taking the plunge, people usually stop and take photographs. Plenty of people come over for a chat. They're curious about what we're doing here and even more curious about what the Chook Chaser is doing here. As soon as I tell them I am going to ride it across the river, they are all too keen to supply a free coaching session. Across the board the advice is to go slow and steady. Just don't open the throttle when you hit a bump or make an unexpected move. One guy advises me to first walk through it to assess the situation. Saltwater crocodiles have been seen in the area, so I'm a bit apprehensive about this idea. But deciding at last that it's better to know what I'm taking my beloved bike through, I decide to make the walk.

The water comes up to my knees. In some places it even rises over my knees. I'm not that tall, but that's still a good forty centimetres, enough to swallow the wheels of the Chook Chaser two-thirds of the way up. No matter which way I approach it, this is properly nerve-wracking.

I haven't felt this nervous since my very first figure-skating competition many, many years ago. Back then my trembling knees and shaky balance put my ass on the ice twice. A similar outcome today would likely destroy the engine. It would get us stuck here on this remote dirt road with a broken bike and it might ruin the chance of any Asian adventures. Seated on the stationary bike I close my eyes and visualise, again and again, the appropriate responses that I will need to make when crossing the river. *Don't open the throttle. Just keep going.* Over and over I visualise myself making it across safely. This makes me feel slightly better, yet my heart still beats at three times its normal pace.

By 3.30 p.m. the water has dropped a significant five centimetres. By 4 p.m. it has dropped a little more. The wind starts to pick up. It feels like a sign. I have to go now.

Lisette crosses the fingers of one hand and holds the camera in the other. I check my gloves, adjust my helmet. I line the bike up at a perfect ninety-degree angle with the water, then take a deep breath and away I go. The first bit isn't deep at all, just rocky, a piece of cake. But about halfway across the water level starts rising. The bike has some serious drag with the panniers in the water. Instinctively I pull my feet up, tell myself, *Keep breathing, slow and steady, slow and steady.* There are big boulders hiding under the black water. The bike is jumping all over the place. I remind myself not to open the throttle. The engine is roaring and screaming in first gear. *I'm sorry my poor Chook Chaser. Just hold on a bit longer.* My eyes are fixed on the bank, my mind working overtime. *Whatever you do, don't open the throttle. You're halfway there. Come on, you can do this!*

With ten metres to go the water level begins to fall. But then the front wheel bounces off something big and the bike tilts dangerously to the right. *Don't open the throttle. Eyes on the prize.* Miraculously we manage to stay upright. As I ride up the bank I shout out my loudest and deepest victory cry. 'Woooohooooo!' This has been by far the hardest, most nerve-wracking thing I've ever done in my life.

Lisette carefully drives Jack through. We party, hug each other and jump up and down when we are both safely across. After all the suspense of the day, I don't feel like riding anymore. We camp close by and watch the sun set over the Pentecost River. The river we've studied, feared, discussed and dreaded. Putting it behind us is an achievement to be proud of.

The next day we leave the Gibb River Road and make our way to Kununurra. Here I find a much-needed replacement for my rear tyre and fix up some other things on the bike. Once this is done we head for the last jewel of nature on our trip: Kakadu National Park.

Kakadu is World Heritage listed for both its natural grandeur and living Indigenous culture. The park organises free guided tours. We are lucky enough to be guided by an incredibly passionate ranger, Christian, who, in a way that is both entertaining and informative, educates us about local Indigenous life. The people here, we learn, still speak their original language. They also retain a wealth of knowledge about nature and traditional tribal practices. We watch two Indigenous women teach a group of tourists their age-old weaving technique. Of the group, only two tourists are able to split one pandanus leaf, which are used to weave with, in an hour. The women, highly amused, split thirty leaves per minute. For Lisette and me it is a greatly humbling experience to learn from them and spend time on their land.

The culture is interesting, special and beautiful, but what is a national park without wildlife? On one of our walks I'm caught up watching some average-looking bird when Lisette suddenly yells, 'Croc!'

I don't believe her, of course, and reply, 'Yeah, right, you're joking.'

'No, *really!*' she insists, in a voice that's both urgent and convincing.

She'll be right!

I look over at the river and, some twenty metres away, I see him, a saltwater crocodile roughly four metres long, the real deal, quietly floating by in the muddy brown water. We stand rooted to the spot, gazing in awe. Strangely I don't feel scared at all, possibly because the creature's slow and languid movements convey an impression of tranquillity rather than threat. Moments pass in which nothing happens and time seems to slow down. Then, suddenly, we come to our senses and, pulling out our cameras, click away wildly to capture this special encounter.

Unfortunately, that night we are confronted with a completely different, more obnoxious type of animal: the mosquito. There are millions and millions of them. More than either of us has ever seen. While we're cooking they bite right through our pants. They show complete disregard for the bug spray we've covered ourselves in. Lisette seems to be in some sort of Zen state and isn't worried about them. But all through dinner I'm frantically jumping up and down, taking wild swings at them and hitting myself, just to kill one biting bugger in the process.

After all this time in the wild, camping and riding, we are quite in sync with nature. We wake up at sunrise and know what time it is simply by looking at the position of that massive ball of fire. We are not surprised by bats flying past at lightning speed around sunset, and we know the cockatoos will become quiet when the bats wake up. All of this is now part of our world, our life and our routine. But I will never, ever be relaxed and in sync with mosquitoes.

After a night of mozzie wrestling, we're excited to visit the 'bathroom' with the best view of our trip. This series of rock pools at the top of a waterfall are one of the highlights of the park. After a short climb, we jump in the water and enjoy the skyscraper-like panorama over the intense green colours of Kakadu. As she floats about Lisette looks at me and says, 'This life thing...'

'Yes, it's hard! Really, really hard!' I continue, concluding her sentence, the sarcasm in my voice flowing over the edge of the rock pool and out over the treetops.

Shortly after this we visit Ubir. This is a historical site with several impressive natural galleries covered in Aboriginal rock art more than ten thousand years old. It's also a great spot to watch the sun setting over the plains. The colours of the sky are incredible – almost as incredible as the number of people fighting over the best spot to take a selfie. We watch the civilised people of the 21st century. They are more concerned with taking the best photo, preferably of themselves, than with enjoying the show that nature and the

Aboriginal artists have put on for us.

We soon grow tired of this and look for a quieter spot, where we sit down and simply appreciate the moment. I don't take any photos, just absorb the experience. It's a deliberate decision. I sense an inexplicable divide between myself and the other people here. I can't level with them, and I certainly don't understand them. Maybe it's because Lisette and I have been alone together so often these last few weeks and have established this connection with the natural world, but it could also be that we are simply very different.

What the people are doing here makes me sick. They are so self-absorbed and superficial that it's horrifying. I don't ever want to be anything like this. Lisette sits quietly beside me. I have the feeling that she too feels disconnected from, and disgusted with, the people that surround us with their petty concerns. Both the place and the moment are magical. Yet everyone is so busy with themselves and their next Facebook status that they miss the special little things.

For me this is a defining moment. It seems I have been following the masses for years, without ever feeling like I've fitted in.

In this quiet place where we sit I observe the way the clouds change shape, the spread of pink and orange colour across the sky. I hear the birds stop singing at the exact moment the sun disappears below the horizon. And I feel an indescribable urge to set myself apart from other people. Not because they don't accept me, but because I decide I want to be different. Now and in the future, I feel this burning desire to separate myself from the masses. How that will look in the future I am unable to foresee. For now, though, it means taking no photos and instead allow this intense, beautiful, colourful moment to become seared into my memory as a marker and reminder of my deliberate choice to stop trying to fit in.

Chapter 15

Destination Darwin

A week or two ago I posted on the Horizons Unlimited motorbike travel website asking whether anyone knew of a cheap and safe place to store a bike for six weeks. Because we've been travelling out of range of the internet, I've had to wait until we reached Darwin to get a reply, but fortunately there is good news. A local biker has offered to store my loyal steed for the agreeable price of a carton of beer. David answers the phone after two rings and becomes extremely excited when I politely explain who I am and why I call.

'Happy to hear from you. I was expecting your call earlier,' he says, before asking in a matter-of-fact way, 'So you're staying over?'

'Ah, well, actually, we are kind of camping somewhere, maybe...'

David's response combines the enthusiasm of a child

on Xmas morning with the down-to-earth logic of a typical Australian. 'Well then go get your stuff,' he bellows down the phone. 'You're staying over here now. And you're not vegetarian, right?' he continues, still in this happy child's voice. 'That's good cause we'll be having a barbeque party. Welcome to Darwin!'

An hour later we turn into the driveway where two men are waiting for us. Dave turns out to be a middle-aged Darwin local. After shaking our hands he shows us around his property and appoints a spot where he tells Lisette to park Jack. The other guy is our age, tall and dark haired, a German who introduces himself as Stefan. He tells us how, over the last year, he rode his Yamaha Ténéré from Germany to Darwin.

Soon we're all holding stubbies of Coopers Mild Ale, which Dave tells us is the only beer he will drink. The stories start as the beer goes down and before long we're joined by a couple of Dave's bike-riding friends, a man named Wayne and a Dutch girl called Ilse. As the steaks sizzle on the barbeque Lisette and I share our outback experiences. Dave and Wayne are impressed by our courage and declare that making a trip like ours is a little insane.

'It would take Australian men a couple of years to prepare for a trip like that,' says Dave, and everyone laughs, while Lisette and I feel proud of our accomplishment.

Stefan adds to the wealth of stories with his crazy experiences in Asia and Ilse and Lisette find out they have mutual friends in the Netherlands. It quickly becomes one of those unforgettable nights. It is the best welcome to Darwin we could have imagined.

We stay with Dave another two days. Lisette sets out to be a true tourist, snapping pics of the city's highlights, while I busy myself getting the paperwork for the bike organised. Time races by and, before we know it, we have to leave again.

On our last night, to thank Dave for his hospitality, Lisette and I prepare a true feast as a farewell dinner. We've eaten well in the desert, but have missed having luxuries like fridges and ovens at our disposal. Now, with Dave's fully-stocked kitchen to work with, we go a little crazy. We prepare a mighty lasagne and, for dessert, make genuine *appelflappen*, which is a Dutch speciality not unlike apple strudel. The food is received with high praise and after we've finished not a single scrap is left.

The next morning we say goodbye to Stefan and Dave and set out for Brisbane, some 3,500 kilometres away. After ten months together it feels strange leaving the

Chook Chaser behind, although I soon learn to appreciate the comfy front seat in Jack. Lisette insists on driving the entire way, although I offer to share. It's her trip, she tells me, and her achievement to go around Australia. It's an argument I both appreciate and totally understand, judging from my own stubbornness. On the road to Brisbane, we camp again every night and have our only shower in one of the hot springs along the way. Little of interest appears along the road, so we just keep driving along the endless, straight, empty roads.

Chapter 16

Torn in Two

Back in Brisbane it takes a while to readjust to normal life. I move in with Lisette for a few weeks and work many hours at the university. It feels great to be back, but in no time at all I'm leaving again. On my last day my colleagues, led by Lisette, organise a surprise farewell party. During these moments I can't help questioning my decision to go travelling in Asia. Here, with these amazing people, a job I love and opportunities to grow in the future. *Why do I follow the call of adventure? Don't I have everything I could ever desire?*

Every Friday afternoon I take the train to the Sunshine Coast. As I watch the sun sink behind the pointy shapes of the Glass House Mountains, I miss my bike intensely. On arrival I meet up with Mike and we spend the weekend together. We go on crazy dates, hikes and runs, and make lasting memories. Not long after I arrived back in Brisbane he asked me to plan nothing for my last weekend in Australia. He's super secretive about it, refusing to tell me where we are going, or even what I should bring with me.

When *the weekend* finally arrives, he hands me a blindfold.

'Put it on,' he says.

I can't help laughing. 'You don't seriously want me to wear this, do you?' I say. 'I'll get car sick and vomit all over the place'

My complaints fall on deaf ears. 'Just put it on and think of something else besides vomiting,' Mike laughs. 'Don't worry. You'll be fine.'

I love the suspense and the slight sense of danger that the blindfold conveys. Slipping it over my eyes I allow myself to be willingly kidnapped. I know I can trust Mike. I know he always has my best interests at heart. It has always been like this, ever since we met, and I know it will stay the same as long as we play a part in each other's lives. It is the purest, least selfish, definition of love.

Meanwhile my inner compass says we are heading to the airport. Indeed, not much later we arrive there. I'm allowed to see where I'm walking, but ordered to stay away from the check-in desk. Since a blindfold at the security check will raise suspicions, my eyesight is returned to me until we pass through that.

Mike is clearly enjoying the way his plans are coming together. He slips the blindfold over my eyes again and guides me through the departure hall to the gate. Here he stops me ten centimetres short of walking into a flight attendant. He is crazy, the blindfold is nuts and I'm both for simply playing along. But these are our memories in the making. Who knows what will happen when I leave Australia? In the end, our memories and the crazy stories we share are the only things we can take with us.

The last few steps to the gate I walk blinded, guided, with a big smile on my face. I can't believe how things have unfolded in my life. Once seated the captain announces the weather forecast for the destination of this secretive weekend, the only Australian state still on my list: Tasmania.

We arrive in Hobart to find that the weather is freezing. It's the coldest place I have ever been in Australia. The conditions are ideal for cuddling up and being close and intimate together. We go for walks around the harbour and visit Port Arthur, the site of a former convict settlement. On the second day it snows and we climb a hill, overlooking the city, where we build a snowman and take crazy pictures of ourselves posing with it. As we both love cooking, we visit the local market, picking up supplies that we take back to our Airbnb townhouse where we cook delicious meals. We avoid restaurants because we want to be alone with each other. In the townhouse we dress up as if for fancy dates and eat in front of a roaring fire. Everything we do feels phenomenal because we are together. This time of enjoying each other's company feels so perfect and vital and I know I will remember it forever. We rarely talk about our impending separation, focusing instead on the present and these precious moments.

At the end of the weekend we fly back to Brisbane. We have three hours to kill between landing and me zooming back into the air on my flight to Darwin. This doesn't leave much time for lengthy goodbyes or sentimental declarations of love. Yet Mike has one more trick up his sleeve. He has decided that to distract ourselves from our impending separation we should jump into go-karts and race around for a bit. I couldn't agree more, finding flying around a track so much more fun than the usual teary 'I'll miss you' confessions we might otherwise face.

After all, what's the point in stating the obvious if all it does is make you sad?

She'll be right!

In our enthusiasm we overdo it in the go-karts and I end up running dangerously late for my flight. Mike floors the accelerator in the car as if he were still on the track. Arriving at the airport we hardly have time for anything more than one last passionate kiss.

'I'll miss you,' I say, looking into his steel-blue eyes, which become misty as my own tear up.

'I'll miss you, too,' says Mike, the corners of his mouth curling up into a small, comforting smile, as if to assure me that everything will be fine.

I have to run then, looking back once over my shoulder to see Mike standing beside his car. He waves and does his best to look happy, but I know that inside he's falling apart just as much as I am.

Dave picks me up from the airport in Darwin. I'm staying with him before starting my nomad life in Asia. When I see my bike again I'm in awe. Wayne promised to make aluminium panniers and a top box for it. It's like my little Chook Chaser grew up. It's a fully-grown adult, a true adventure bike, complete with its first stickers. After giving the bike a good clean and a last little tinker, it is ready for Asia.

Unfortunately the same thing can't be said about the paperwork. Taking a motorbike overseas isn't easy. It involves a lot of bureaucratic hassle and, when things go wrong, some headaches too. In a few short weeks I make numerous phone calls and send a heap of emails to the shipping company. Sometimes they respond, sometimes they don't. It appears these hurdles are just part of the adventure. Then word comes through that the Carnet de Passage, a sort of passport for the bike, is ready to be picked up in Darwin. But when I check it, I find some major mistakes. With only three days before the bike sails, a new carnet has to be printed and sent from Canberra, at the other end of the country.

My last few days in Australia are an emotional rollercoaster. I'm stressed about the carnet, but feel better when I spend time with Dave and Stefan. Dave's place, which he jokingly calls 'Junglebum's Biker Bunker' forms the bridge between Australia and Asia. It's a comfort to be able to chill out there in between racing around performing all the tasks I have to accomplish before flying out.

I know it's going to be hard to leave all my friends. But on the other hand I feel this incredible pull within and a deep excitement about travelling in Asia. It's an inherent part of travelling to leave people and things behind. But I haven't understood yet why following my heart means losing Mike. *To experience the new, do you really have to go through these conflicting emotions?* Some days I think how lovely it would be if I could just pack him away in a box with my nice shoes, my old laptop and my special dress, so he would be there to come back to when the call of adventure is satisfied and I'm ready to stay still for a while.

On shipping day I find myself nervously holding the phone in my right hand, crossing the fingers of my left. *Please let it be here, please let it be here.* The lady on the other end of the line delivers good news. As if by a miracle, the carnet has only just arrived. When I go to collect it I find that it's perfect, without a single mistake.

Dave accompanies me to customs. It's the first of many, many customs checks on the upcoming trip. A friendly officer looks over the bike. As a final check he asks me to point out the engine number. Getting down on my knees, I study the engine. *Where is the number?* Feeling increasingly stupid I walk from one side of the bike to the other and back. The uniformed man finds it all extremely amusing. He crosses his arms and leans back to enjoy my bewilderment.

Oh my, how will I ever navigate an entire continent if I can't even locate the engine number on my own bike?

Dave steps in and helps with the quest. In no time at

all he locates the number, nicely tucked away on top of the engine, where it is barely visible. After the paperwork is stamped we make our way to the harbour and deliver the bike to the shipping company. Here the Chook Chaser must be weighed to determine the shipping costs.

Amazingly, however, there are no scales that fit a motorbike. To fix this shortcoming a rugged Aussie tradesman is summoned. With his big, calloused hands he grabs the rear wheel and lifts it. He then walks to the front, grabs the front wheel and lifts that. Little drops of sweat sit on his smiling upper lip as he looks at me and states in the most Australian of accents, 'Ah, 'bout a hundred kg, I reckon.' With that, it is settled.

Anticipating our upcoming separation, I run my fingers over the Chook Chaser one last time. 'Thank you for carrying me across this country, little bike,' I say. 'If all goes well we will be reunited in East Timor in a few weeks.'

With most of the stress out of the way, excitement about the future takes over. A new continent awaits, with new people, new languages, new adventures. However, it is hard to believe that I'm really leaving Australia, the country that for the last two years has provided a warm, welcoming home to me. The great experiences I've had here, and the amazing people I've met, have taught me the life lessons I needed to learn in order to pursue my journey. It is because of everything Australia has given me that I've decided to continue travelling with the Chook Chaser. So as much as it hurts to leave, it's time to move on. It's time to take this adventure to the next level.

To Asia!

Acknowledgements

There are many people without who, this book would not have been written or published. To all of you I am eternally grateful. It is for your support, guidance, wisdom and motivation that I was able to complete the journey, find the inspiration to write and the courage to get this book published.

First of all, thank you to my parents Inge and Ton Simons. From a very young age you have always encouraged me to make my own decisions. You taught me to assess my own abilities and if needed, strengthen them. You taught me to push my limits, do what makes me happy and follow my heart. You are at the base of who I am, and who I will grow in to be. This book is me in words and spirit, and it wouldn't have been possible without you by my side.

It's now fitting to give massive credit to my travel buddy Lisette Bakker. Oh my, did you have no idea what you were getting yourself into when we set off together. We've seen the best and the worst of each other while we made lifetime memories. The intensity of our shared time created a bond that will be there forever. Your down to earth, let's get on with it mentality is a jewel of a trait. Many times when writing this book, dwelling on what to write, waiting for inspiration to strike, I'd think back to our days in the desert. I'd remember how you would jump out of bed in the morning, no snoozing, into the cold air, and you would have breakfast ready before I found the motivation to open my eyes. You're a goal-kicker and an eternal glass-half-full optimist, I can only hope a little bit of that has rubbed off on me.

When it comes to inspiration I don't have to go far from home, it was my brother Dimitri Simons, who once and for all showed me that anything is possible when you commit to it. When he first told me he planned to sail solo across the Atlantic Ocean I had no doubt in my mind he would. Two years later he did. He has given me the belief that it can be done, inspiring me to ride many miles and write thousands of words.

Truus Simons and Mieke Uten, my grandmas thank you for your patience and understanding while this crazy granddaughter of yours set out to conquer the world. Your support upon return to the Netherlands gave me the space I needed to complete this book.

Through all these kilometres of empty roads, intense romances and endless life purpose monologues there was one person who kept me sane. Lilla Hollo, my best friend. No matter how many time zones there were between us, I could call you in the middle of the

Acknowledgements

night when on the verge of a mental breakdown. Your simple wisdom kept my thoughts in check both during the journey and long after. You understand my crazy brain better than I do!

This leads me to thank the people who made this journey so unforgettable that I wrote a book about it. First of all Andrew, Belle and Nadine. Your advice got me on the road and you gave me the leads to keep going. Aurelio, the Yamaha salesman and my virtual housemate, who's enthusiasm and support travelled with me across the planet. Matt and Dario for creating intense and unforgettable memories together. Thank you to my housemate Lisa, for your caring friendship, for cucumber with sesame oil & salt and for the surf and yoga sessions. You made your world my home. Then, I would never have considered writing a book if it wasn't for Amy. You were the first one to make me realise some stories are worth sharing with a bigger audience. Thanks to Scotty and David who both gave me a place to stay, a bit more comfortable than my leaky tent. Of course this journey would not have been possible without the financial means. So a special thank you goes out to my university supervisors Liz Bradshaw and Gert-Jan Pepping. You allowed me to teach, one of my all time passions, even though I wasn't sure if I'd stay around for longer than a semester.

Last but not least, I have to thank the man who turned my world upside down. The one who came after me and then let me go, even when he probably wanted me to stay. The man who always pushed me to be more of myself, encouraged me to keep going when things got tough and taught me where to look for the wisdom I needed to find. He is the one who encouraged me to grow as a person and trail blaze through life. The man who loved me and I loved him, in the most pure and selfless way. Thank you Mike for being the person you are and for inviting me to be part of your life.

Credit

There are a few people, whose support has shaped this book coming into existence in a special way. Danielle Martel, from Created by Danielle, fellow motorcycle traveller and the engine behind my website and graphics. Esther Holland, who as a coach helped me find the right mindset to write. Thank you for believing in my story and giving me mental tools to put it together.

To contact these amazing women:
Danielle Martel: createdbydanielle.com
Esther Holland:
    www.linkedin.com/in/esthersfcoach
    www.facebook.com/EstherHollandCoaching/
    esthersf.coach@gmail.com

Thank you Ian Robert Smith, my editor, for complying with my ridiculous timeframes and for making this book 100% better while keeping its original tone and spirit. Thanks to Nathan Millward for educating me about the life of a writer. As well as a massive thumbs up to all the people on the next page who had enough faith in this book to read it ahead of publication and share it with their friends and followers.

She'll be right!

Lisette Bakker
Morné Terblanche
Amy Sorensen
Sofie Jacobs
Ruud Adegeest
Roger and Laura Younger
David Parsons
Hein Schwartz
Andy Greager
Nigel Caughey
Steve Hamilton
David Wright
Linda Sebihi
Dimitri Simons
Annelies Voordendag
Kylie Thomas
Barbara Kalkman
Marije ter Sluis
Irene Roos
Ilse Blokland
Chiel van de Steeg
Bart van Veen
Bob Radder
Rainer Janssen
Tim Helm
Sarah Kashyap
Bhavna Sharma
Hema Choudhary
Adriana Hinestrosa

Credit

Santanu Banerjee
Lilla Hollo
Mirelle Dol
Rainer Janssen
Marcel van Dijken
Simon Visser
Ruth Belcher
Job Boers
Merina Shrestha Casper
Sue Barnes
Marie Fontenau
Bas Hillerstrom
Marieke Boot
Jilmil Kakoti Buyan

Printed in Great Britain
by Amazon